Internet of E
and Big

T0074483

Internet of Everything (IoE)

Series Editor: Mangey Ram, Professor, Graphic Era University, Uttarakhand, India

IoT
Security and Privacy Paradigm
Edited by Souvik Pal, Vicente Garcia Diaz, and Dac-Nhuong Le

Smart Innovation of Web of Things
Edited by Vijender Kumar Solanki, Raghvendra Kumar and Le Hoang Son

Big Data, IoT, and Machine Learning
Tools and Applications
Rashmi Agrawal, Marcin Paprzycki, and Neha Gupta

Internet of Everything and Big Data
Major Challenges in Smart Cities
Edited by Salah-ddine Krit, Mohamed Elhoseny, Valentina Emilia Balas, Rachid Benlamri, and Marius M. Balas

Bitcoin and Blockchain
History and Current Applications
Edited by Sandeep Kumar Panda, Ahmed A. Elngar, Valentina Emilia Balas, and Mohammed Kayed

For more information about this series, please visit: https://www.crcpress.com/Internet-of-Everything-IoE-Security-and-Privacy-Paradigm/book-series/CRCIOESPP

Internet of Everything and Big Data

Major Challenges in Smart Cities

Edited by

Salah-ddine Krit, Mohamed Elhoseny,
Valentina Emilia Balas, Rachid Benlamri,
and Marius M. Balas

CRC Press
Taylor & Francis Group
Boca Raton London New York

CRC Press is an imprint of the
Taylor & Francis Group, an **informa** business

CRC Press
Boca Raton and London
First edition published in 2022
by CRC Press
6000 Broken Sound Parkway NW, Suite 300, Boca Raton, FL 33487-2742
and by CRC Press
2 Park Square, Milton Park, Abingdon, Oxon, OX14 4RN

Library of Congress Cataloging-in-Publication Data

Names: Krit, Salah-ddine, editor. | Elhoseny, Mohamed, editor. | Balas, Valentina Emilia, editor. | Benlamri, Rachid, editor.
Title: Internet of everything and big data : major challenges in smart cities / edited by Salah-ddine Krit, Mohamed Elhoseny, Valentina Emilia Balas, Rachid Benlamri, and Marius M. Balas.
Description: First edition. | Boca Raton, FL : CRC Press, 2020. | Series: Internet of Everything (IOE). Security and privacy paradigm | Includes bibliographical references and index.
Identifiers: LCCN 2020016636 (print) | LCCN 2020016637 (ebook) | ISBN 9780367458881 (hardback) | ISBN 9781003038412 (ebook)
Subjects: LCSH: Smart cities. | Internet of things. | Big data.
Classification: LCC TD159.4 .I54 2020 (print) | LCC TD159.4 (ebook) | DDC 307.760285/4678--dc23
LC record available at https://lccn.loc.gov/2020016636
LC ebook record available at https://lccn.loc.gov/2020016637

ISBN: 978-0-367-45888-1 (hbk)
ISBN: 978-1-003-03841-2 (ebk)

Typeset in Times LT Std
by KnowledgeWorks Global Ltd.

Contents

Preface

The motivation for this book stemmed from the fact that there are currently no in-depth books dedicated to the challenge of the Internet of Everything and Big Data technologies in smart cities.

The world today is confronting a critical portability challenge, and the framework that moves cities must keep pace with the innovation. This book reviews the applications, technologies, standards, and other issues related to smart cities. Smart cities have been an area of concern for both academic and industrial researchers. Big Data and Internet of Everything technologies are considered the most significant topics in creating smart cities. Wireless sensor networks are at the heart of this concept, and their development is a key issue if such a concept is to achieve its full potential. This book is dedicated to addressing the major challenges in realizing smart cities and sensing platforms in the era of Big Data cities and the Internet of Everything. Challenges vary from cost and energy efficiency to availability and service quality.

This book examines the challenges of advancing Big Data and the Internet of Everything. The focus of this volume is to bring all the new idea- and application-related advances into a single work, so that undergraduate and postgraduate students, analysts, academicians, and industry experts can effectively understand the high-quality techniques related to IoT and Big Data.

Editors

Salah-ddine Krit, PhD, is an Associate Professor at the Polydisciplinary Faculty of Ouarzazate, Ibn Zohr University, Agadir, Morocco. He is currently the Director of Engineering Science and Energies Laboratory and the Chief of Department of Mathematics, Informatics and Management. Dr. Krit earned his PhD degrees in Software Engineering from Sidi Mohammed Ben Abdellah University, Fez, Morocco, in 2004 and 2009, respectively. From 2002 to 2008, he worked as an engineering team leader in audio and power management integrated circuits (ICs) research, design, simulation, and layout of analog and digital blocks dedicated to mobile phone and satellite communication systems using Cadence, Eldo, Orcad, and VHDL-AMS technology. Dr. Krit has authored/coauthored more than 130 journal articles, conference proceedings, and book chapters. His research interests include wireless sensor networks, network security, smart homes, smart cities, Internet of Things, business intelligence, Big Data, digital money, microelectronics, and renewable energies.

Mohamed Elhoseny, PhD, is an Assistant Professor at the Faculty of Computers and Information, Mansoura University and a researcher at CoVIS Lab, Department of Computer Science and Engineering, University of North Texas. He is the Director of Distributed Sensing and Intelligent Systems Lab, Mansoura University, Egypt. Collectively, Dr. Elhoseny has authored or coauthored more than 100 ISI journal articles, conference proceedings, book chapters, and nine books. His research interests include sensor technologies, network security, Internet of Things, and artificial intelligence applications. Dr. Elhoseny serves as the Editor-in-Chief of the *International Journal of Smart Sensor Technologies and Applications,* IGI Global. He also is an associate editor of other prestigious journals.

Valentina Emilia Balas, PhD, earned her PhD in Automation and Applied Informatics at Aurel Vlaicu, University of Arad, Romania. She is a Professor at Aurel Vlaicu, University of Arad, Romania. Dr. Balas is the author of more than 265 research papers. Her research interests are in intelligent systems, fuzzy control, and soft computing.

Rachid Benlamri, PhD, is a Professor of Software Engineering at Lakehead University, Canada. He earned his master's degree and PhD in Computer Science from the University of Manchester, United Kingdom, in 1987 and 1990, respectively. He is the head of the Artificial Intelligence and Data Science Lab at Lakehead University. He has supervised more than 80 students and postdoctoral fellows. He served as a keynote speaker and general chair for many international conferences. Prof. Benlamri is a member of the editorial board for many refereed international journals. His research interests are in the areas of artificial intelligence, semantic web, data science, ubiquitous computing, and mobile knowledge management.

Marius M. Balas, PhD, is a Professor in the Department of Automatics and Applied Software at the Faculty of Engineering, University Aurel Vlaicu, Arad, Romania. He holds a Doctorate in Applied Electronics and Telecommunications from the Politehnica University of Timisoara. Prof. Balas is an IEEE Senior Member. He is the author of 4 books, 12 book chapters, more than 100 papers (33 ISI/BDI papers, 40 papers in journals and conference proceedings, etc.), and 7 invention patents. His research interests are in electronic circuits, modeling and simulation, adaptive control, intelligent and fuzzy systems, soft computing, and intelligent transportation. The main original concepts introduced by Prof. Balas are fuzzy interpolative systems, passive greenhouse, constant time to collision optimization of the traffic, imposed distance braking, internal model bronze casting, PWM inverter for railway coaches in tropical environments, rejection of the switching controllers effect by phase trajectory analysis, and the Fermat neuron. He has been a mentor to many student research teams and challenges, and has received awards from Microsoft Imagine Cup, GDF Suez, etc. He has participated in many international conferences as an organizer and session chair, and has been a member in international program committees. Prof. Balas is editor-in-chief, member of editorial board, or reviewer for several international journals.

Contributors

Kaoutar Aamali
Research and Engineering Laboratory
National High School for Electricity
and Mechanics
Casablanca, Morocco

Ahmed Abbou
Department of Electrical Engineering
Mohammed V University
Rabat, Morocco

Hajji Abdelghani
Mohammedia School of Engineering
Mohamed V University
Rabat, Morocco

El Boukili Abdellah
Higher Education School
Mohamed V University
Rabat, Morocco

Khalid Abouloula
Department of Mathematics,
Informatics and Management
Ibn Zohr University
Agadir, Morocco

Abdelhakim Alali
Research and Engineering Laboratory
National High School for Electricity
and Mechanics
Casablanca, Morocco

Mohammed Alaoui
Research Team in Thermal and Energy
ENSET, Mohammed V University
Rabat, Morocco

Nouar Aoun
Unité de Recherche en Energies
renouvelables en Milieu Saharien
(UERMS)
Centre de Développement des Energies
Renouvelables
Adrar, Algeria

Abdeldjabar Babahadj
Unité de Recherche en Energies
renouvelables en Milieu Saharien
(UERMS)
Centre de Développement des Energies
Renouvelables
Adrar, Algeria

Abdellah Bah
Research Team in Thermal and Energy
ENSET, Mohammed V University
Rabat, Morocco

Marius M. Balas
Department of Automation and Applied
Software
Aurel Vlaicu University of Arad
Arad, Romania

Valentina Emilia Balas
Department of Automation and Applied
Software
Aurel Vlaicu University of Arad
Arad, Romania

Mebrouk Bellaoui
Unité de Recherche en Energies
renouvelables en Milieu Saharien
(UERMS)
Centre de Développement des Energies
Renouvelables
Adrar, Algeria

Yousra Berguig
Systems and Optimization Laboratory
Ibn Tofail University
Kenitra, Morocco

Kada Bouchouicha
Unité de Recherche en Energies
    renouvelables en Milieu Saharien
    (UERMS)
Centre de Développement des Energies
    Renouvelables
Adrar, Algeria

Malak Bouhazzama
Department of Strategies and
    Governance of Organizations
National School of Management
Tangier, Morocco

Abdellah Boussafi
IMMII Laboratory
Hassan 1st University
Settat, Morocco

Zineb Cabrane
Department of Electrical Engineering
Mohammed V University
Rabat, Morocco

Daoui Driss
Ibn Tofail University
Kenitra, Morocco

Mohamed Elhoseny
Mansoura University
Dakahlia, Egypt

Hajar Hafs
Research Team in Thermal and Energy
ENSET, Mohammed V University
Rabat, Morocco

Sanae Hanaoui
Systems and Optimization Laboratory
Ibn Tofail University
Kenitra, Morocco

Zineb El Hariti
Research and Engineering Laboratory
National High School for Electricity
    and Mechanics
Casablanca, Morocco

Laassiri Jalal
Informatics Systems and Optimization
    Laboratory
Ibn Tofail University
Kenitra, Morocco

Muhammad Shoaib Khan
Department of Economics
Shah Abdul Latif University
Khairpur Mirs, Sindh, Pakistan

Salah-ddine Krit
Department of Mathematics,
    Informatics and Management
Ibn Zohr University
Agadir, Morocco

Jalal Laassiri
Systems and Optimization Laboratory
Ibn Tofail University
Kenitra, Morocco

Saloua Marhraoui
Department of Electrical Engineering
Mohammed V University
Rabat, Morocco

Abdellah Mechaqrane
Laboratory of Renewable Energies and
    Smart Systems
Sidi Mohamed Ben Abdellah
    University
Fez, Morocco

El Hammoumi Mohammed
Industrial Laboratory Techniques
FST, Sidi Mohammed Ben Abdellah
    University (USMBA)
Fez, Morocco

Said Mssassi
Department of Strategies and
　Governance of Organizations
National School of Management
Tangier, Morocco

Najat Ouaaline
IMMII Laboratory
Hassan 1st University
Settat, Morocco

Ibrahim Oulimar
Unité de Recherche en Energies
　renouvelables en Milieu Saharien
　(UERMS)
Centre de Développement des Energies
　Renouvelables
Adrar, Algeria

Nadir Oumayma
Financial Markets Department
Ibn Tofail University
Kenitra, Morocco

Ali Ou-Yassine
Department of Mathematics,
　Informatics and Management
Ibn Zohr University
Agadir, Morocco

Muhammad Saleem Rahpoto
Department of Economics
University of Sindh
Jamshoro, Sindh, Pakistan

Mohamed Sadik
Research and Engineering Laboratory
National High School for Electricity
　and Mechanics
Casablanca, Morocco

Lahrizi Sara
Informatics Systems and Optimization
　Laboratory
Ibn Tofail University
Kenitra, Morocco

Parveen Shah
Department of Economics
Shah Abdul Latif University
Khairpur Mirs, Sindh, Pakistan

Subir Sinha
Lecturer (SACT), Department
　of Journalism and Mass
　Communication
Dum Dum Motijheel College
[Affiliated under West Bengal State
　University], India

Urooj Talpur
Department of Economics
Shah Abdul Latif University
Khairpur Mirs, Sindh, Pakistan

Nibareke Thérence
Informatics Systems and Optimization
　Laboratory
Ibn Tofail University
Kenitra, Morocco

Ech-Chelfi Wiame
Industrial Laboratory Techniques
FST, Sidi Mohammed Ben Abdellah
　University (USMBA)
Fez, Morocco

Anass Zaaoumi
Research Team in Thermal and Energy
ENSET, Mohammed V University
Rabat, Morocco

1 Analytical Review of Roles of the Internet in the Indian Education System

Subir Sinha

Dum Dum Motijheel College, West Bengal University, India

CONTENTS

1.1 INTRODUCTION

India, a South Asian developing nation with a huge population, is rapidly rising as a responsible global superpower. The nation is maintaining a secular approach with multiple vernacular languages. Imparting education and information dissemination are becoming a challenging factor in this vast populated nation, but the government has overcome the issue through the use of mass media. Mass media is helping to impart an education and to disseminate information in a successful way, but the rise of the Internet and digitalization has caused this to happen at an even faster pace. In the last few decades, various sectors have experienced development. India is focusing on multiple sectors, but the prime focus is on information and communication

1

technologies and the education system. Education and information exchange are a top priority in India. Education has been important in India since the Vedic age, but with the arrival of the modern age, the education system has become modernized. The government and private organizations have introduced various initiatives to modernize the education system. The main objective is to promote knowledge and education for social development. The government and private organizations are instructing the educational institutes to use the latest technologies for demonstration and learning. In the 1990s, the Indian government utilized mass media, such as radio and television, for mass education and they organized programs like SITE, the Kheda communication project, and the Radio Rural Forum. But with the arrival of the Internet, the system has changed. In the present circumstances, the government and its education department are motivating educational institutes and teachers to use modern technologies such as computers, the Internet, and projectors for presentations along with class lectures for demonstration and learning. The mission and vision of the education system are to disseminate education and learning among the citizens of India in a new way.

The Internet is playing a key role in this process. The use of the Internet is multidimensional and makes the field of information transmission democratic. It provides a wide range of valuable information and data to the citizens of India. They are free to search and read any information according to their needs using various search engines and web browsers. The Internet is helping them to gain information and knowledge and transforming the Indian education system into a global platform. The Internet gives everyone the opportunity to access and learn any information according to his or her choice and need. Now, students can also access various e-books for their education. The rise of Wikipedia, the free encyclopedia, is a wonderful case study that reveals the access of information through the Internet. This multilingual, web-based, free encyclopedia was launched in 2001 by Jimmy Wales and Larry Sanger. It serves students and the general public globally by providing a huge source of information. Thus, Indian education systems are benefitting a great deal from the use of the Internet.

In the age of globalization, people have accepted Internet browsing as a daily habit, and surfing the Internet has become a kind of addiction for the new generation. The Internet has both pros and cons. It is helping to promote a global educational culture and has led to the rapid pace of globalization. In higher studies, students and scholars can easily access various materials and research data from across the globe through the Internet. They can even share their own work by uploading it to various websites. Thus, the Internet provides a means to not just acquire knowledge but also make connections with others. Through the Internet, we can talk with anybody about any topic. The e-learning facilities the Internet enables are highly valuable for the progress of the Indian education system.

1.2   THE INTERNET AS A HUGE SOURCE OF INFORMATION

The emergence of the Internet has brought a revolution to the information and education system. Scholars and students who are surfing the Internet are mainly getting three types of information and data: educational or study material, formal information, and informal information. Through the Internet, Indian students and scholars also have access to digital e-libraries, which play a vital role in the modern education system. Various educational institutes and organizations are delivering valuable formal information regarding admissions, examinations, registration, fee structure, scholarships, etc., through their websites via the Internet. In terms of the education system, formal information means the authentic organized message, notice, or tender published by the educational institutes or government organizations. This information is highly dependable and trustworthy in nature and is necessary for the progress of the education system in India. The Internet also provides information that is informal in character, and its authenticity and validity are less important in nature compared to formal information.

1.3   SOCIAL MEDIA AND THE EDUCATION SYSTEM

Social media is not only used for the dissemination of news or to promote social relationships, it is also used for the promotion of education. Indian students and scholars greatly favor social media for their education. Social networking sites such as Facebook support students and educators by delivering relevant information. For example, Facebook provides the platform to create groups where various educators, scholars, and students can join as members and post data and information. They can discuss various subjects in a coordinated fashion, which leads to better outcomes in terms of education. In addition, Facebook users can select and "like" various web portals where they receive data and information related to formal and informal education. Social media for them serves as a platform where they can cooperate and share information and knowledge. The users can post various video clips along with photographs and graphical representations to the web portal for the betterment of the education system and the educators.

YouTube is another video sharing site that provides various video clips related to formal and informal education. It teaches viewers proper demonstration and provides illustrations. Viewers can select videos to watch according to their need; they can pause and rewind the video clips. It is a very user-friendly site and tries to provide full satisfaction to users through its videos.

Another social networking site, WhatsApp, is hugely popular and is also helping in terms of education and information transmission. Students, scholars, and educators can easily transfer any information, data, video, or photographs to their classmates or to any educator within a very short span of time. Students and educators can create groups, and only the group admin has the capacity to select group members. WhatsApp attracts many students and educators because of its easy functioning and video calling features.

1.4   THE INTERNET AND THE GOVERNMENT'S EDUCATIONAL ORGANIZATION

The government and higher education departments are taking various initiatives for the propagation of knowledge and mass education. They are trying to put education in a modern dimension, and technologies are facilitating this for the education system by providing modern outlook. In India, both central and state governments use various websites for the development of the education system. The websites help with information dissemination, coordination, and propagation of modern teaching policies.[1]

An organization such as the University Grants Commission, which became a statutory organization of the government of India by an act of Parliament in 1956, has the main aim of the coordination, determination, maintenance of standard teaching, examination, and research in university education. It also has a website for information dissemination. Although various state governments have formed their own boards and councils for educational purposes, they are also disseminating formal information through their own websites. These organizations are disseminating various notices, circulars, and orders; various schemes; and several scholarship programs for students and scholars through their websites. Information about seminars, conferences, and research activities are also available.

Recently, the government of India under the Honorable Prime Minister Narendra Modi initiated a policy called "Digital India."[2] The Digital India program is a flagship program of the government of India, with a vision to transform India into a digitally empowered society and knowledge economy. To this end, Digital India has introduced several initiatives taken by both public and private sectors such as I Share for India, e-Pathshala, e-basta, and Nand Ghar, which will impart education using technologies including smart phones, mobile apps, and Internet services in remote areas where it may not be possible for teachers to be present in person. The power of technology cannot be denied. It is expected that delivering education through this digital platform to children and teachers could be a potential way to bridge the education deficit.

1.4.1 CASE STUDY: THE NATIONAL CONFERENCE OF ICT AND "I SHARE FOR INDIA" INITIATIVE OF THE GOVERNMENT OF INDIA, MINISTRY OF HUMAN RESOURCE DEVELOPMENT

In India, the Ministry of Human Resource delivers various schemes, publishes various reports, issues various notices and orders, etc. Among these, the case study about a scheme called "I Share for India" cannot be ignored. The Narendra Modi government's policy of Digital India influenced the Human Resource Development (HRD) ministry to launch a number of mobile apps and web-based platforms allowing students to access study materials online and parents to keep track of the performance and attendance.[3] During the National Conference on ICT (on July 11, 2015), the Honorable Human Resource Minister announced the initiative of "I Share for India" inviting interested groups, agencies, organizations, and community members to participate in the creation of an educational resources pool for school and teacher education. The program is totally Internet and website based.[4] Smriti Irani, the Human Resource Minister of India, told reporters, while speaking about the initiatives, "We are trying to leverage technology not only to bring more transparency in school education system but also to create new learning opportunities for the children."

1.5   THE INTERNET AND DIGITAL LEARNING

The Internet and new media are also providing Indian students with digital or e-learning facilities. In most cases, this refers to courses, programs, or degrees that are taught completely online. Students can utilize electronic technologies such as computers and the Internet to access an educational curriculum, instead of going to a traditional classroom. High priorities are given to curriculum-based subjects such as literature, science, and economics. This is highly effective in imparting meaningful education to the students. It is one of the most modernized forms of learning systems and is playing a significant role in various parts of India.

A digital e-learning platform overcomes the barriers of geographical and cultural boundaries, allowing teachers to bring knowledge beyond the classroom, potentially to a worldwide audience. Students and young aspirants from all around the world can attend and contribute to lessons, creating global conversations through so many different points of view on the same topic, with the result of an enriched educational experience. In various research projects, digital learning helps the researcher as a form of valuable secondary data. Online education has proven to be highly beneficial recently. Utilization of higher education through online courses to a vast majority of students not only provides a mass education but also generates a huge source of revenue for the education department.

1.5.1   CASE STUDY: THE "VIRTUAL CLASS" OF INDIRA GANDHI NATIONAL OPEN UNIVERSITY

Indira Gandhi National Open University (IGNOU),[5] established by an act of Parliament in 1985, has continuously striven to build an inclusive knowledge society through inclusive education. It has tried to increase the gross enrollment ratio (GER) by offering high-quality teaching through the open and distance learning (ODL) model. Recently, through the Internet, IGNOU has organized a "virtual class," an e-learning platform developed to deliver an online program. The platform provides a complete online experience, from registration to certification.

1.6   THE INTERNET AND DIGITAL LIBRARIES

Reading books and magazines enriches the reader's mind and heart with knowledge and wisdom. Reading is one of the oldest habits of human civilization. The emergence of the Internet has created an extraordinary change in reading culture by providing digital libraries. A digital library is a collection of data, books, magazine, various valuable manuscripts, or any kind of published material in an organized electronic form. They can be accessed through various websites via the Internet. Digital libraries vary in size and scope. They have changed the system where users do not need to visit a physical library to access its reference collection.

1.6.1 CASE STUDY: E-PATHSHALA OF NCERT

E-Pathshala[6] was developed by NCERT for showcasing and disseminating all educational e-resources, including textbooks, audio, video, periodicals, and a variety of other print and nonprint materials, through a website and mobile app. The platform addresses the dual challenge of reaching out to a diverse clientele and bridging the digital divide (geographical, sociocultural, and linguistic), offering comparable quality of e-contents, and ensuring free access anytime, anywhere. All the concerned stakeholders such as students, teachers, educators, and parents can access e-books through multiple technology platforms, that is mobile phones (Android, iOS, and Windows platforms) and tablets (as e-publications) and on the web through laptops and desktops (as flipbooks).

All the NCERT books have been digitized and uploaded. Currently the e-contents are available in Hindi, English, and Urdu. The states and the union territories are being approached to digitize and share all textbooks in Indian languages through this platform, which will be done in a phased manner. The web portal and mobile app of e-Pathshala were launched by Honorable HRM during the National Conference on ICT in School Education on November 7, 2015.

1.7 CONCLUSION

The dawn of the twenty-first century has shown the rapid growth of the Internet in India. The education sector in India has long awaited an overhaul to meet the growing demand for a contemporary education system that is accessible to all. In the last decade, children and youth in India have become increasingly technology driven, revealing considerable potential and readiness to learn using digital media. The uses of the Internet are proving beneficial for Indian citizens. The support of the Internet in the education system is enormous. It is acting as a powerful tool of information dissemination, while on the other hand diffusing knowledge and education among the masses for the welfare of society. It is also helping to minimize the digital divide. It has proved to be a highly valuable networking system for students and scholars, acting as a mass educator. The Internet has provided Indian scholars access to digital learning, where students can take courses through the computer. Digital libraries (e-libraries) are also helping students access books and published materials directly through the Internet. The central government and various state governments are also taking various initiatives to propagate knowledge and information through websites. The Indian central government under the Honorable Prime Minister Narendra Modi initiated the policy of "Digital India." The government of India launched this program with the vision to transform India into a digitally empowered society and knowledge economy. The policy of Digital India highlights the process of digitalization in various sectors. In the education system, initiatives like "I Share for India" and "E-Pathshala" are the result. Clearly the Internet has placed India and its education system on a global path.

REFERENCES

1. https://www.ugc.ac.in/
2. https://www.digitalindia.gov.in/
3. https://mhrd.gov.in/ICT-Initiatives-I-share-for-India
4. Govt launches many mobile apps as part of Digital India initiative; By Press Trust of India 08.Nov.2015. https://yourstory.com/2015/11/digital-india-mobile-apps?utm_pageloadtype=scroll
5. Preamble; http://www.ignou.ac.in/ignou/aboutignou/profile/2
6. https://mhrd.gov.in/ICT-Initiatives-e-Pathshala

2 Performance Evaluation of Components of the Hadoop Ecosystem

Nibareke Thérence, Laassiri Jalal,
and Lahrizi Sara
Ibn Tofail University, Kenitra, Morocco

CONTENTS

2.1 INTRODUCTION

Currently, people are expressing their thoughts through online blogs, discussion forms, and some online applications such as Facebook and Twitter. If we take Twitter as an example, almost 1 TB of text data is generated in one week as tweets [1].

The tweets can be categorized based on the hash value tags for which people comment and post their tweets [2]. Big Data brings the challenge of storage and processing to obtain a competitive advantage in the global digital market [3]. Hadoop fills this gap by providing storage and computing capabilities for huge data effectively. It consists of a distributed file system, and it offers a way to parallelize and execute programs on a cluster of machines [4, 5].

In this chapter, we run a word processing application on Hadoop MapReduce, Pig, and Hive on a single node under Ubuntu and compare the performance. The chapter is organized as follows: Section 1 introduces the work, the objective, and the description of the proposed system; section 2 is a background study; section 3 presents the model and the experimental environment; section 4 presents some scripts performed and the results on processing applications with MapReduce; and section 5, discusses the results; the chapter is concluded in section 6.

2.1.1 OBJECTIVE

Twitter has more than a billion users, and every day billions of tweets are generated and this number is constantly increasing [6, 7]. To analyze and understand the activity occurring on such a scale, a relational SQL database is not enough. This type of data is well suited to a massively parallel and distributed system [8] such as Hadoop. Our main goal is to focus on how data generated from Twitter can be used by different companies to make targeted, real-time, and informed decisions about their product and then compare the performance of Hadoop ecosystem tools.

2.1.2 PROPOSED SYSTEM

The main challenge of Big Data is related to storage and access of information from the large number of cluster datasets [9]. We need a standard platform to manage Big Data as data volume increases and data are stored in different locations in a centralized system, thus reducing the huge amount of data in Big Data.

The second challenge is to extract data from large sets of social media data. In scenarios where data are increasing daily [10], it is somewhat difficult to access data from large networks if you want to perform a specific action. The third challenge is designing an algorithm to deal with the problems posed by the huge volume of data and their dynamic characteristics.

The main goal of this chapter is to extract and analyze the tweets and perform sentiment analysis to determine the polarity of tweets and the most popular hashtags displaying the trends and determine the average ranking of each tweet according to topic using different analysis tools.

2.2 BACKGROUND STUDY

In the last few years, the Internet is more widely used than ever. Billions of people are using social media and social networking sites every day all across the globe [10]. Such a huge number of people generates a flood of data, which has become quite complex to manage. Considering this enormous amount of data, a term has been coined to represent it: Big Data [11]. Big Data has an impact in various areas of life all over the world.

2.2.1 Big Data

As mentioned, data that are very large in size and yet growing exponentially with time are called Big Data [12]. They may be structured or unstructured and make use of certain new technologies and techniques. Hadoop is a programing framework that is used to support the processing of large datasets in a distributed computing environment. It provides storage for a large volume of data, along with advanced processing power [13]. It also gives the ability to handle multiple tasks and jobs. Hadoop was developed by Google's MapReduce, which is a software framework where an application is broken down into various parts. The Apache Hadoop ecosystem consists of the Hadoop Kernel; MapReduce; Hadoop Distributed File System (HDFS) [11]; and a number of various other components like Apache Flume, Apache Hive, and Apache Pig, which are used in this project.

Data from different sources can be found in many structures [14, 15]:

- *Structured data*: Data that can be stored and processed in a table (rows and columns) format are called structured data. Structured data are relatively simple to enter, store, and analyze. Example—Relational database management system.
- *Unstructured data*: Data with an unknown form or structure are called unstructured data. They are difficult for nontechnical users and data analysts to understand and process. Example—Text files, images, videos, emails, web pages, PDF files, PowerPoint presentations, social media data, etc.
- *Semi-structured data*: Semi-structured data refers to neither raw data nor data organized in a rational model like a table. XML and JSON documents are semi-structured documents.

2.2.2 Characteristics of Big Data

The characteristics of Big Data are defined mainly by the three Vs [15, 16]:

- *Volume*: This refers to the amount of data that is generated. The data can be low density, high volume, structured/unstructured, or with an unknown value. The data can range from terabytes to petabytes.
- *Velocity*: This refers to the rate at which the data are generated. The data are received at an unprecedented speed and are acted upon in a timely manner.
- *Variety*: Variety refers to different formats of data. They may be structured, unstructured, or semi-structured. The data can be audio, video, text, or email.

2.2.3 Hadoop

As organizations are getting flooded with massive amounts of raw data, the challenge is that traditional tools are poorly equipped to deal with the scale and complexity. That is where Hadoop comes in. Hadoop is well suited to meet many Big Data challenges, especially with high volumes of data and data with a variety of structures [16, 17]. Hadoop is a framework for storing data on large clusters of everyday computer hardware that is affordable and easily available and running applications against that data. A cluster is a group of interconnected computers (known as nodes) that can work together on the same problem. As mentioned, the current Apache Hadoop ecosystem consists of the Hadoop Kernel; MapReduce [18]; HDFS; and a number of various components like Apache Hive, Pig, Flume, etc.

Hadoop consists of two main components: HDFS (data storage) and MapReduce (data analysis and processing). Hadoop can run over Linux or Windows operating system. Actually, there are many versions of Hadoop. Figure 2.1 shows the Hadoop ecosystem and its components.

HDFS is a distributed file storage system that splits a file into many blocks. Each block is replicated into different nodes. The replication factor can be configured in the Hadoop node. HDFS is written in Java and developed by Apache. It is a fault-tolerant file system that can allow for a restore when a node crashes [17].

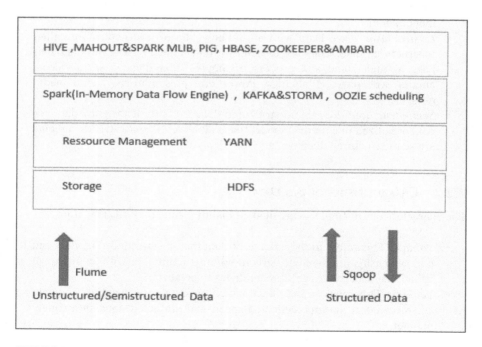

FIGURE 2.1   Hadoop architecture.

YARN (Yet Another Resource Negotiator) is responsible for resource management in a Hadoop node. It also helps in job scheduling and execution on different nodes of the Hadoop cluster [17, 19].

MapReduce is a processing paradigm that consists of two functions: Map and Reduce. The Map function splits a file into list of keys and values [19]. The Reduce function combines a list of key and value elements into a single output using aggregation.

2.3   OUR MODEL WORKFLOW

2.3.1   WORK PROCESS

To retrieve real-time tweets on data, we used Apache Flume, and to store those large volumes of Twitter data, we used HDFS. After storing the data, we performed sentiment analysis on Twitter data using MapReduce, using the distributed cache concept to implement sentiment analysis [20].

2.3.2   PROPOSED METHODOLOGY

Our algorithm uses the following steps: We first create a Twitter account; then we can use the Twitter application programming interfaces (APIs) to retrieve data in real time; we can recover the data using Apache Flume, through which we can make an API call to the Twitter database that starts to retrieve the data (Figure. 2.2).

We need to be able to store these real-time data reliably. So, we use HDFS. After storing the data in HDFS, we can process the data using Hadoop MapReduce; after treatment, we can begin to analyze this large amount of social data and compare

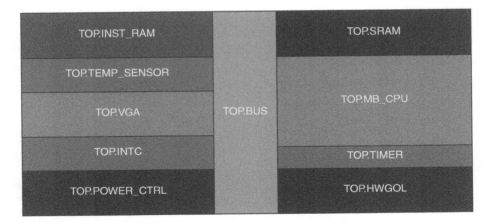

FIGURE 2.2   The proposed model workflow.

FIGURE 2.3 Tweets analysis workflow.

the MapReduce treatment with Pig, as well as Pig with Hive, in terms of performance. Figure 2.3 shows the workflow of analyzing tweets.

2.3.3 EXPERIMENTAL TOOLS CONFIGURATION

Table 2.1 presents the main hardware and software features of the system.

Regarding the software settings, the evaluations used a stable version of Hadoop. The infrastructures were configured based on usage and system characteristics (number of processor cores and memory size, for example). The MapReduce algorithm was implemented on a system using Hadoop 3.0.0 and Eclipse IDE 3.0 Ubuntu 8.2. Table 2.2 shows the most important parameters of the configuration.

In our experiment, we performed analysis on the tweets using MapReduce, Pig, and Hive, and we compared the performance of the three tools. The steps were as follows:

- Create a Twitter application.
- Get data using Apache Flume.
- Analyze data with Hadoop MapReduce.
- Conduct a study on the performance of the Hadoop framework and its components (Pig and Hive).

TABLE 2.1

Node Configuration

Hardware Configuration
CPU Intel® Core™ i5
CPU Speed 2.5 GHz
#Cores 4
Memory 3.6 GB
Disk 30 GB
Software Configuration
OS version Linux Ubuntu 18.04
Kernel Linux 5.0.0-29-generic x86_64
Java Open JDK 64 bit-server VM (build 25.222.b10, mixed mode)

TABLE 2.2
Framework Configuration

Hadoop
HDFS block size: 128 MB
Replication factor: 3
Number of under-replication blocks: 8
Minimum allocation memory: 1024, vCores: 4
Maximum allocation memory: 8192, vCores: 4
MapReduce
Worker per node: 1
Worker cores: 4
Mapreduce.map.java.opts: Xmx1024M

2.4 IMPLEMENTATION

2.4.1 GET DATA USING APACHE FLUME

Apache Flume is a distributed, reliable, and available service that collects, aggregates, and efficiently transfers large amounts of streaming data [21] to HDFS. It can be used to transfer Twitter data into the Hadoop HDFS [22].

After creating an application on the Twitter development site, we want to use the consumer key and the secret key, as well as the access token and the secret values, by which we can access Twitter and get the information that exactly matches what we want here; we will get everything in JSON format. This information is stored in the HDFS file that we have specified to record all data from Twitter. The configuration file contains all the details needed to configure the Flume agent that ingests data continuously from various data sources and transmits it to HDFS. Figure 2.4 shows the configuration of our Flume file.

To collect and store the Twitter dataset in HDFS, we performed the following steps:

- Start all Hadoop start-all.sh services. Then check all the Hadoop services that work by using the jps command.
- Start the channel agent using the following command:*/usr/lib/flume/bin/ flume-ng agent −conf ./conf/-f/usr/lib/flume/conf/flume.conf Dflume.root. logger=DEBUG,console-n TwitterAgentDtwitter4j.streamBaseURL = https://stream.twitter.com/1.1/*

2.4.2 ANALYSIS USING HADOOP MAPREDUCE

After retrieving and storing Twitter data in HDFS, we can begin our analysis using MapReduce. As mentioned, MapReduce is a powerful framework for processing large distributed sets of structured and unstructured data on a Hadoop cluster stored in the HDFS.

```
# Naming the components on the current agent.
TwitterAgent.sources = Twitter
TwitterAgent.channels = MemChannel
TwitterAgent.sinks = HDFS

# Describing/Configuring the source
TwitterAgent.sources.Twitter.type =
org.apache.flume.source.twitter.TwitterSource
TwitterAgent.sources.Twitter.consumerKey = Your OAuth consumer
key
TwitterAgent.sources.Twitter.consumerSecret = Your OAuth consumer
secret
TwitterAgent.sources.Twitter.accessToken = Your OAuth consumer
key access token
TwitterAgent.sources.Twitter.accessTokenSecret = Your OAuth
consumer key access token secret
TwitterAgent.sources.Twitter.keywords = tutorials point,java,
bigdata, mapreduce, mahout, hbase, nosql

# Describing/Configuring the sink
TwitterAgent.sinks.HDFS.type = hdfs
TwitterAgent.sinks.HDFS.hdfs.path =
hdfs://localhost:9000/user/Hadoop/twitter_data/
TwitterAgent.sinks.HDFS.hdfs.fileType = DataStream
TwitterAgent.sinks.HDFS.hdfs.writeFormat = Text
TwitterAgent.sinks.HDFS.hdfs.batchSize = 1000
TwitterAgent.sinks.HDFS.hdfs.rollSize = 0
TwitterAgent.sinks.HDFS.hdfs.rollCount = 10000

# Describing/Configuring the channel
TwitterAgent.channels.MemChannel.type = memory
TwitterAgent.channels.MemChannel.capacity = 10000
TwitterAgent.channels.MemChannel.transactionCapacity = 100

# Binding the source and sink to the channel
TwitterAgent.sources.Twitter.channels = MemChannel
TwitterAgent.sinks.HDFS.channel = MemChannel
```

FIGURE 2.4   Flume configuration file.

To perform sentiment analysis on Twitter data using MapReduce, we will use the concept of distributed caching. The following are the three steps to perform sentiment analysis:

- *Implementation of distributed caching*: Using the distributed cache, we can perform side joins (Map). We will therefore join the dictionary dataset containing the sentiment values of each word. In order to carry out the sentiment analysis, we will use a dictionary called AFINN.

AFINN is a dictionary composed of 2500 words classified between +5 and −5, depending on their meaning. In MapReduce, map-side joins are performed by the distributed cache. The distributed cache is applied when we have two datasets, where the smallest size is limited to the cluster cache. Here, the dictionary is the smallest dataset, so we use the distributed cache.

- *Write a mapper class to calculate the feelings*: The Map method takes each record as input, and the record is converted to a string using the toString method. After that, we created a jsonobject called jsonparser, which parses each record in JSON format and then extracts the tweet_id and tweet_text that are required for sentiment analysis. In the Reduce class, we just pass the mapper input as output.
- *Write a driver class for our MapReduce program and implement distributed caching*: In the driver class, we must provide the path to the cached dataset. The result of sentiment analysis with MapReduce is shown in Figure 2.5.

```
433099539201806336    "@Nathan_lamoreB: Shake and bake"     ----> 0
43309956235833456     We lost an amazing dog and a best friend today. I will miss you so much Abby. http://t.co/fLihtMwuhJ  ----> 2
43309957065400256     RT @Petco: Who can resist Tiwaz the Swedish Vallhund? He even volunteers at a local school. Truly a great dog!
#wKCDogShow http://t.co/Wwpr..  ----> 3
43309958498293862     @obrientopron OH YM DOG YES WE WOULD WONX TAHN SI HAPPENING THEN     ----> 0
43309958706719539     DIY SayItWithLOVE Dog Treat Jar #WilkBoneLOVE http://t.co/x145VeSVVg via @SugarTheGoldenR    ----> 0
43309959437783649     @TifffanyParsons grow it out!!  ----> 0
43309959837922508     RT @callmeswagur: Rt disd better close I gotta wash my dog    ----> 2
43309960487281996     RT @RichelleDBeadle: Dog show judges are so fancy.  Like eating candy bars with knife and fork fancy. I'm
intimidated.    ----> 0
43309960502341222     So @CRonohr.....     ----> 0
43309961658742886     Am I the only one that crackers help when feeling sick ??    ----> 1
43309962648558888     RT @BeautifulStary: This dog's owner is trapped inside and his dog is trying his best to help him http://t.co/
tno92f7hei    ----> 3
43309963761313792     @jordanflood51 this is pretty great☺ http://t.co/480cIV4FzC   ----> 1
43309964419361406     "@carlo_drewski: I just made a deep fried hamburger....don't ask me why"why ?   ----> 0
43309966302186291     RT @itsMovieSecrets: The dog from Air Bud passed away today.    ----> 0
43309966623467110     When your boyfriend pretends to get a phone call from his dog just to get out of hanging out with
you&lt;&lt;&lt;&lt;&lt;    ----> -1
43309967802526105     My dog and I have seen literally THOUSANDS of movies together :')    ----> 0
43309970538850304     When your dog takes up half the bed &lt;&lt;&lt;&lt;&lt;&lt;&lt;&lt; #moveitorloseit    ----> 0
43309970544343440     you can't teach a old dog new tricks but you can teach a old bitch how da trick a new trick ☺  ----> -5
43309971507356467     Be the person your dog thinks you are.   ----> 0
43309973681694401     RT @Pupplesgonwild: RIP to the dog that played air bud☺ http://t.co/CljNlsGarj    ----> 0
43309973681448960     RT @MONLIEROZAY: "@HsTRILLADIAMOND: It's a dog eat dog world"

EAT OR GET DEVOURED !    ----> 0
43309975612738764     I hate you, like I really freakin hate you!    ----> -4
43309977718563148     @DeintolTeo @desnoadkon @mlsw7 cb date a dog just so you can say you are not alone HAHA might as well date our dog la,
@donluuffyy  ----> -2
43309978141984896     RT @TheSportsHernia: This dog is a blatant asshole and sleeps in a nicer bed than you on the Upper East Side. http://
t.co/yGXQ6S9zfq ----> -4
43309980762687782     RT @itsMovieSecrets: The dog from Air Bud passed away today.   ----> 0
43309981561981465     "@Yo_Vilches: Kill these bitches when I feel like it. ☺"   ----> -3
43309984052059750     I want love like that. ☺    ----> 0
```

FIGURE 2.5   Tweets with their polarity score.

2.4.3 PERFORMANCE COMPARISON BETWEEN MAPREDUCE AND PIG

As part of the performance study, we can perform a Pig analysis similar to that of MapReduce, which is performed on preprocessed data.

- 20 MB of data were used on the Twitter form.
- The two tools are very accurate in terms of calculating the feeling score, but there is a difference in processing time between the two images; Figure 2.6 shows the execution time taken by the two images.

Apache Pig needs 15 seconds to run, but the MapReduce programing model only takes 10 seconds to analyze the feeling score of a file size of 20 MB of data (Figure 2.6). We saw a 2 percent improvement in the tools using the formula:

$$(\text{OLD} - \text{NEW})\,/\,\text{OLD} \times 100 = (15 - 10)\,/\,15 \times 100 \qquad (2.1)$$

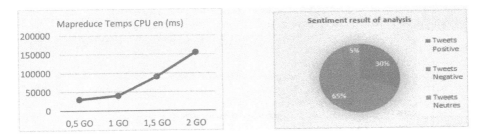

FIGURE 2.6   Tweets analysis.

MapReduce's performance was 33.33 percent more than that of Pig. Thus we can conclude that MapReduce is better than the Pig for analyzing polarity and Twitter feeling scores.

2.4.4 PERFORMANCE COMPARISON BETWEEN PIG AND HIVE

Pig is a high-level language for data transformation that analyzes data as a data stream. This language is an abstraction of the programing of the MapReduce model, which makes it an high level query language (HLQL) built on Hadoop. It includes many traditional data operations (sorting, joining, filtering, etc.), as well as the ability for programmers to develop their own data access, processing, and analysis functions. Pig provides an engine for running parallel data streams using the Hadoop framework.

The Pig architecture shows that Pig Latin scripts are first handled by the parser, which checks the syntax and instance of the script. The output of the parser is a logical plane, a collection of vertices where each vertex executes a fragment of the script. Pig provides poor performance compared to Hive when conducting the performance test.

The queries performed show that the execution time taken by Hive is much shorter than that of Pig, and the reduction of the Map generated by Hive is less numerous than that of Pig. The experiment has shown that Hive works faster compared to Pig on the basis of various parameters (request, number of lines of code, and execution time).

For analyzing sentiment analysis on tweets with Apache Pig using the AFINN dictionary, we used the following script. The Hive script used for sentiment analysis on tweets was as follows.

```
// Add Jars
REGISTER '/home/kiran/Desktop/elephant-bird-hadoop
compat-4.1.jar';
REGISTER '/home/kiran/Desktop/elephant-bird-pig-4.1
REGISTER '/home/kiran/Desktop/json-simple-1.1.1.jar';
load_tweets = LOAD '/user/flume/tweets/' USING
com.twitter.elephantbird.pig.load.JsonLoader('-nestedLc
AS myMap;
// Extraire l'identifiant et le hashtag des tweets
extract_details = FOREACH load_tweets GENERATE
myMap#'id' as id,myMap#'text' as text;
tokens = foreach extract_details generate id,text,
FLATTEN(TOKENIZE(text)) As word;
dictionary = load '/AFINN.txt' using PigStorage('\t')
AS(word:chararray,rating:int);
word_rating = join tokens by word left outer, dictionary
word using 'replicated';
// describe word_rating;
rating = foreach word_rating generate tokens::id as
id,tokens::text as text, dictionary::rating as rate;
word_group = group rating by (id,text);
avg_rate = foreach word_group generate group,
AVG(rating.rate) as tweet_rating;
positive_tweets = filter avg_rate by tweet_rating>=0;
```

Continued

Continued

```
create external table load_tweets(id BIGINT,text STRING)
ROW FORMAT SERDE
'com.cloudera.hive.serde.JSONSerDe' LOCATION
'/user/flume/tweets'
create table split_words as select id as id,split(text,' ') as words
from load_tweets;
create table tweet_word as select id as id,word from
split_words LATERAL VIEW explode(words) w as word;
lateralView: LATERAL VIEW udtf(expression) tableAlias AS
columnAlias (',' columnAlias)*fromClause: FROM baseTable
(lateralView)
create table dictionary(word string,rating int) ROW FORMAT
DELIMITED FIELDS TERMINATED BY '\t';
LOAD DATA INPATH '/AFINN.txt' into TABLE dictionary;
create table word_join as select
tweet_word.id,tweet_word.word,dictionary.rating from
tweet_word LEFT OUTER JOIN dictionary
ON(tweet_word.word =dictionary.word);
select id,AVG (rating) as rating from word_join GROUP BY
word_join.id order by rating DESC;
```

2.5 RESULTS AND DISCUSSION

The MapReduce-based Hadoop components provide a better understanding of pro-graming language perspectives, such as the ease of programing and configuration to link to the Hadoop runtime environment. This conciseness is a yardstick to see how expressive the two components based on MapReduce (Hive and Pig) are to deter-mine if they provide more abstract languages.

After performing operations on Twitter data using Pig and Hive, we can now perform a comparative analysis, considering the total running time of the hashtag-counting scripts and the average tweets score. In our experience, we have found that Hive is more powerful than Pig when analyzing datasets (Figure 2.7). This is the

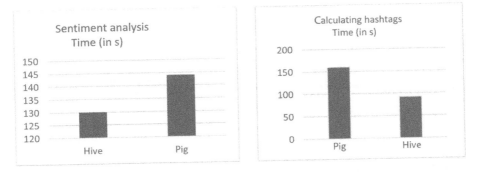

FIGURE 2.7 Performance in counting tweet hashtags.

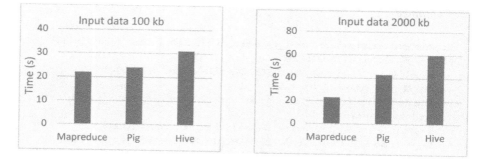

FIGURE 2.8   Execution time taken by the two components of the Hadoop ecosystem.

case according to various parameters, be it in the hashtag count test or in the sentiment analysis test. The queries also show that the execution time taken by Hive is much shorter than that obtained with Pig (Figure 2.9).

MapReduce tasks generated by Hive are less numerous than those of Pig, the execution time being shorter in Hive. Another benefit of using Hive is the number of lines of code, which are more in Pig, but in Hive, a single-query line is enough. The experimental results are shown in Figure 2.9.

In most tests, Pig shows the same performance when increasing the input size (Figure 2.9). Although its rate of source code metric is high compared to Hive, we can say that Hive offers performances close to those of Big SQL.

If we write applications with MapReduce and execute them, we get better performance. The Latin Pig language offers data flow programmers the opportunity to work with Hadoop.

The executions of the word count test using MapReduce, Pig, and Pig with two different sizes of data types (text files) returned the following results, as shown in Figure 2.9: Hive provides a query language similar to SQL for querying all files stored on HDFS. Pig provides a scripting language that can be used to transform the data. The Hive and Pig languages are converted to Java MapReduce programs

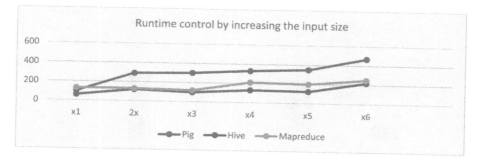

FIGURE 2.9   Runtime control by increasing the input size.

before being submitted to Hadoop for processing. Java MapReduce programs can be written to customize input formats or perform specific functions available in Java.

The execution of Latin Pig and HiveQL instructions takes longer than native MapReduce processing because they are ultimately translated into MapReduce tasks. The flexibility of Pig Latin and Hive is achieved at the expense of performance.

With sentiment analysis, the characteristic to study is the total execution time, which increases with the input size. We can see that MapReduce Java and Hive clearly get better results, as shown in Figure 2.8: While the Hive queries reach the most powerful processing time of the three experiments, Pig takes longer for sentiment analysis queries.

2.6 CONCLUSION

The analysis of large data is not only important but also necessary. In fact, many organizations that have implemented Big Data are gaining a significant competitive advantage over other organizations without Big Data efforts. Our project aimed to analyze Big Data on Twitter and provide insight information. Twitter posts can be an important source of opinions on different issues and topics. This can give us a precise idea of the subject and can be a good source of analysis. In our work, we performed sentiment analysis to determine the polarity of a tweet based on the AFINN dictionary. The results show that MapReduce is an efficient paradigm for the analysis of Twitter data. The Pig and Hive instructions simplify the syntax of the queries and decrease the Java MapReduce code. However, the flexibility of Pig and Hive is achieved at the expense of performance. We conducted tests on separate data (tweets, text files) using different methods. In our future work, we will test other sources of data to see if performance depends on the data type we have to analyze. We also will experiment other models in order to improve the performance of Big Data tools.

REFERENCES

[1] Inoubli, W., Aridhi, S., Mezni, H., Maddouri, M., and Mephu Nguifo, E. «An experimental survey on big data frameworks». *Future Generation Computer Systems*, vol. 86, p. 546–564, Sept. 2018. https://linkinghub.elsevier.com/retrieve/pii/S0167739X17327450.

[2] Mangal, N., Niyogi, R., and Milani, A. Analysis of users' interest based on tweets. In: International Conference on Computational Science and Its Applications. Springer, Cham, 2016. https://doi.org/10.1007/978-3-319-42092-9_2.

[3] Zheng, W., Qin, Y., Bugingo, E., Zhang, D., and Chen, Jb. Cost optimization for deadline-aware scheduling of big-data processing jobs on clouds. *Future Generation Computer Systems*, vol. 82, p. 244–255, May 2018. https://doi.org/10.1016/j.future.2017.12.004.

[4] Lu, S., Wei, X., Rao, B., Wang, L., and Wang, L. LADRA: Log-based abnormal task detection and root-cause analysis in big data processing with Spark. *Future Generation Computer Systems*, vol. 95, p. 392–403, June 2019. https://doi.org/10.1016/j.future.2018.12.002.

[5] Nenavath Srinivas, N., Negi, A., Tapas Bapu, B. R., and Anitha, R. A data locality-based scheduler to enhance MapReduce performance in heterogeneous environments. *Future Generation Computer Systems*, vol. 90, p. 423–434, Jan. 2019. https://doi.org/10.1016/j.future.2018.07.043.

[6] Prabowo, R., and Thelwall, M. Sentiment analysis: A combined approach. *Journal of Informetrics*, vol. 3, no 2, p. 143–157, April 2009. https://doi.org/10.1016/j.joi.2009.01.003.

[7] Thelwall, M. The Heart and soul of the web? Sentiment strength detection in the social web with SentiStrength. In: *Cyberemotions*. Springer, Berlin, Germany, 2017. p. 119–134. https://doi.org/10.1007/978-3-319-43639-5_7.

[8] Gurini, D. F., Gasparetti, F., Micarelli, A., and Sansonetti, G. A sentiment-based approach to twitter user recommendation. *RSWeb@ RecSys*, vol. 1066, 2013.

[9] Jayalakshmi, A. N. M., and Krishna Kishore, K. V. Performance evaluation of DNN with other machine learning techniques in a cluster using Apache Spark and MLlib. *Journal of King Saud University-Computer and Information Sciences*, Sept. 2018. https://doi.org/10.1016/j.jksuci.2018.09.022.

[10] Mahdavinejad, M. S., Rezvan, M., Barekatain, M., Adibi, P., Barnaghi, P., and Sheth, A. P. Machine learning for internet of things data analysis: A survey. *Digital Communications and Networks*, vol. 4, no 3, p. 161–175, 2018. https://doi.org/10.1016/j.dcan.2017.10.002.

[11] Uzunkaya, C., Ensari, T., and Kavurucu, Y. Hadoop ecosystem and its analysis on tweets. *Procedia-Social and Behavioral Sciences*, vol. 195, p. 1890–1897, 2015. https://doi.org/10.1016/j.sbspro.2015.06.429.

[12] Feller, E., Ramakrishnan, L., and Morin, C. Performance and energy efficiency of big data applications in cloud environments: A Hadoop case study. *Journal of Parallel and Distributed Computing*, vol. 79, p. 80–89, 2015. https://doi.org/10.1016/j.jpdc.2015.01.001.

[13] Michalik, P., Štofa, J., and Zolotova, I. Concept definition for Big Data architecture in the education system. In: 2014 IEEE 12th International Symposium on Applied Machine Intelligence and Informatics (SAMI). 2014. https://doi.org 10.1109/SAMI.2014.6822433.

[14] Giudice, P. L., Musarella, L., and Sofo, G. An approach to extracting complex knowledge patterns among concepts belonging to structured, semi-structured and unstructured sources in a data lake. *Information Sciences*, vol. 478, p. 606–626, 2019. https://doi.org/10.1016/j.ins.2018.11.052.

[15] Moharm, K. State of the art in big data applications in microgrid: A review. *Advanced Engineering Informatics*, vol. 42, p. 100945, 2019. https://doi.org/10.1016/j.aei.2019.100945.

[16] Zhang, D., Pan, S. L., Yu, J., and Liu, W. Orchestrating big data analytics capability for sustainability: A study of air pollution management in China. *Information & Management*, p. 103231, 2019. https://doi.org/10.1016/j.im.2019.103231.

[17] Mohammed, E. A., Far, B. H., and Naugler, C. Applications of the MapReduce programming framework to clinical big data analysis: Current landscape and future trends. *BioData Mining*, vol. 7, no 1, p. 22, 2014. https://doi.org/10.1186/1756-0381-7-22.

[18] Verma, J. P., and Patel, A. Comparison of MapReduce and spark programming frameworks for big data analytics on HDFS. *International Journal of Computer Science & Communication*, no 2, 2016. https://doi.org/10.090592/IJCSC.2016.113.

[19] Pethuru, R. The Hadoop ecosystem technologies and tools. In: *Advances in Computers*. Elsevier, 2018. p. 279–320. https://doi.org/10.1016/bs.adcom.2017.09.002.

[20] Vinodhini, G., and Chandrasekaran, R. M. Sentiment analysis and opinion mining: A survey. *International Journal*, vol. 2, no 6, p. 282–292, 2012. https://doi.org/10.1016/j.sbspro.2015.06.429.

[21] Rathee, S. Big data and Hadoop with components like Flume, Pig, Hive and Jaql. In: International Conference on Cloud, Big Data and Trust. 2013.

[22] Birjali, M., Beni-Hssane, A., and Erritali, M. Analyzing social media through big data using infosphere biginsights and Apache Flume. *Procedia Computer Science*, vol. 113, p. 280–285, 2017.

3 The Effect of the Financial Crisis on Corporal Wellbeing

Apparent Impact Matters

Muhammad Shoaib Khan[1],
Muhammad Saleem Rahpoto[1], and
Urooj Talpur[2]
[1]Shah Abdul Latif University Khairpur Mirs, Sindh, Pakistan
[2]University of Sindh, Jamshoro, Sindh, Pakistan

CONTENTS

3.1 INTRODUCTION

The worldwide monetary crisis (WMC), which started in late 2006 and proceeded in 2007, remained to a great extent due to the bursting of the real estate bubble as home loan defaults rose in 2006 and prompted a decrease in home values throughout the world. (Jonas et al. 2007). Exchange rates of international transactions created problems in the development section of economies causing budgets to be reviewed and increased gradually at the end of 2008, hence resulting in the losses in the development segment. Here we use a longitudinal informational index, which gives a unique chance to examine the effect of GLOBAL FINANCIAL CRISIS (GFC) in an example of middle-aged and older adults, as information gathering covers the majority of 2006 to the majority of 2012. We remain especially intrigued in how the knowledge of pressure as well as budgetary circumstance Financial Services (F.S.) throughout the WMC time frame can predict physical wellbeing.

Despite the fact that the condition of the world economy doesn't contrast starting with one individual then onto the next, the degree to which such outer conditions influence wellbeing and prosperity relies upon different elements. Bronfenbrenner well depicts this realism in his bioecological (Bronfenbrenner, 1976; Bronfenbrenner and Ceci, 1994); inside these structures, human involvement is an element of the lively communication among people. In Bronfenbrenner's model, the ongoing financial downturn is some portion of a large-scale framework, fusing expansive social and monetary conditions that support increasingly close to home logical elements; we suppose the effect of these full-scale levels occasion on the distinct–and precisely on the corporeal—soundness of the individual to rely upon the abstract or saw understanding of the individual, the deepest degree of Bronfenbrenner's model. The key factors at the individual level here are the view of pressure (PS) and abstract monetary experience during the GFC time frame.

3.2 WELLBEING FINANCIAL ASPECTS AND FUND

Studies show predictable unfavorable impacts of monetary downturns and budgetary strains on physical wellbeing. One investigation found that with expanding joblessness, physical wellbeing decreases in an example of middle-aged adults (French and Davalos, 2011); an alternative distinguishes work security as a significant factor in anticipating corporeal wellbeing in an example of utilized adults, by the individuals who discover their employment to be less steady and secure and report less fortunate wellbeing self-evaluations and more conclusions of interminable ailments (Virtanen et al., 2002). An imminent report found that members confronting constant financial hardship—characterized by the pay level beneath the government destitution line—had fundamentally worse physical working conditions for 10 years or more than the individuals who didn't face such hardship. These creators accentuate the focal point of this discovery, bringing up that the outcomes show little help for the turnaround impact that decreased physical working prompts financial troubles in this example (Lynch et al., 1997). A later report in India finds a comparative impact in which entities living in lower-pay areas—an indicator of manageable monetary pressure—are at higher danger of creating ceaseless wellbeing circumstances than persons in higher-salary areas (Kulkarini, 2012), Fascinatingly, a few examinations show that target markers of physical wellbeing and mortality improve during times of financial downturn, maybe because of a more advantageous ways of life (Gardhem and Rhome, 2005; Neumayer, 2003; Regidor et al., 2013).

3.2.1 WEIGHT ON WELLBEING

PS, or these degrees of tension experienced by a separate wellbeing, have established a solid and steady association with corporeal wellbeing at the cutting edge of writing. More significant heights of apparent pressure remain related by more unfortunate shortened and extended-haul corporeal wellbeing results, counting expanded degrees of cardiac infection (Richardson et al., 2012), diminished resistant capacity

(Godbout and Glaseer, 2005), increased danger of interminable wellbeing situations by and large (Kulkarni, 2013), and a considerably more noteworthy danger of mortality (Nieelsen et al., 2007). These affiliations are usually thought to remain a component of intervened physical pressure reaction, which will in general go with mental pressure (Meerz et al., 2001). Precisely, the writing on allostatic burden indicates that tenacious physical pressure reaction—activated by incessantly elevated levels of PS—prompts "wear" on the body, steadily undermining cardiovascular, metabolic, and resistance capacity and essentially builds the danger of advanced illnesses, for example, diabetes, hypertension, and coronary illness (Juster et al., 2009). Since monetary issues are one of the most habitually referred to wellsprings of PS (American Psychological Association, 2010) and since these are sorts of issues are generally do not settle rapidly and this establish a wellspring of constant pressure, we suppose monetary/money-related connections between the elements and wellbeing discussed earlier are known because of the expanded pressure due to interminable budgetary issues.

3.2.2 THIS INVESTIGATION

Here, we utilize five streams of longitudinal information covering the GFC time frame to inspect how the ongoing monetary downturn has influenced wellbeing in our example; explicitly intra-singular vicissitudes in PS and abstract FS during the past as indicators of wellbeing trying to overcome the restrictions & their desired rule of law and regulations for account of different variations to nutshell the tentative aftershocks on the global financial term as a trademark and treated as the best example of proper investigation behind this whole scenario. Explicit theories for the general example are that advanced PS gauge heights and more prominent pressure increment over the period will anticipate intensifying wellbeing at upsurge 5; that inferior benchmark heights of abstract FS and increasingly critical decreases in FS over the span would foresee exacerbating wellbeing in wave 5; and that when the two variables are considered, the effect of PS will intervene (or at any rate incompletely clarify) the wellbeing impact of FS. Furthermore, we estimate that when these impacts are considered independently for the individuals who encountered a decrease in emotional FS contrasted with the individuals who encountered an improvement, the earlier speculations would just exist in the decreased group; for individuals in the development group, we hope to see an optimistic alteration in FS given medical advantages toward the finish of the study, and we imagine these impacts not to be influenced by feelings of anxiety (which are as yet predictable to contrarily influence wellbeing in that group).

3.2.3 STRATEGY MEMBERS AND TECHNIQUE

Members were 312 adults ages 30 to 70 years on upsurge 1 (M = 54.4), speaking to a subspecies of the bigger Notre Dame 'Healthiness and Wellbeing Education (NDHWB; N = 974), where a longitudinal investigation is proceeding, investigating worry with regards to maturing. So as to get the most relevant test conceivable, NDHWB members are enlisted from a list obtained from a social think-tank dependent on a yearly review of private family units and statistics information. The NDHWB's center segment is a yearly poll bundle that members complete every day and return via postal mail in return for a $20 gift card; here we utilize five wave reviews covering spring 2007 to spring 2013, trying to shoot for models during the GFC. All members consented to take part, and all methodologies were endorsed by the institutional review board of the University of Notre Dame.

To be incorporated into this investigation, members needed to have wellbeing information for wave 01 and wave 05; the individuals who needed information at multiple times (N = 313) would in general be more seasoned (mean contrast of 2 years; p = .008), had lower wages (p = .006), and had somewhat increasingly less training (p = .01) than the individuals who didn't. Two individuals reported no pay and were removed from the examination. From the last example of 312 individuals, all members had at any rate three floods of information; 80% of members (N = 280) had information at all 05 period focuses, 6.4% (N = 21) had information at 04 time focuses, and 3.4% (N = 12) needed information at 03 time focuses. The example was 64% female, predominantly Caucasians (84.5%; the second most common ethnic group was African Americans with 10.5%) and generally accomplished (53% had approximately type of post-school optional training and just 4% had not finished a secondary institute). Half of the members were married, with the remainder separated (27%); 13% are widowed and the remaining 10% report that they are single. There was a noteworthy descent in variety in Wave 1 income, with 5% making <$75,000 yearly, 16% making $75,000 to $149,000 every year, 11% making $15,000 to $24.9,000 yearly, 23% making $25,000 to $39,9000 consistently, 32% making $40,000 to $74.900 every year, and 13% making >$75,000 per year.

3.2.4 MEASURES

Salary: To represent progressively target FS data in logical models, we utilized pay data as a control. At each wave, every member reports their yearly pay as tending to be categorized as one of 07 pay classifications: <US$7.5k, $7.5k to $14.9k, $15k to $24.9k, $25k to $39.9k, $40k to $74.9k, $75k to $99.8k, and ≥$100k. This class is oblique after 01 to 07 and are preserved as a ceaseless variable with advanced notches representing higher pay for an assumed year. The adjustment in pay will be demonstrated when the member's picked pay classification contrasts starting from one year to the next.

Emotional Financial Situation: Subjective FS is estimated utilizing four positions arranged by the Mid-life Growth Study in the United States (MIDUS) (Beim et al., 2006), by the phrasing and configuration of reactions marginally altered to encourage organization. In the NDHWB poll 03 things counted the assessment of present monetary circumstance and ranged from 01 to 10, with advanced scores showing a progressively ideal circumstance; one thing (when all is said in done, which of the announcements later depicts the current budgetary status of you and your family?) had various answers demonstrating whether the member felt that the family had increasingly, enough, or insufficient cash to address certain issues. Every one of the four things corresponded emphatically with one another, and the mean wave dependability factor for these four things on a scale may be 0.72 (range = 0.71

to 0.73). These 04 things remained institutionalized (M = 0, normal nonconformity (S.D) = 01) and added towards shaping a solitary outcome: advanced notches demonstrate healthier F.S.

Seen Tension: These sizes of apparent pressure are measured PS every day (Cohen et al., 1982). These measurements estimate the general degree of tension an individual has encountered in the most recent month; 14 questions asked things like: How regularly did you get agitated about something that happened surprisingly? Also, how regularly have you effectively managed the irritating issues of life? Are evaluated on a 04 opinion scale (01 = not ever, 04 = consistently). Potential notches run from 16 to 58, with advanced scores demonstrating more PS (07 points with turnaround score). A 20% lost information law was applied to the gauge, so when ascertaining the gauge of people who needed 03 or fewer things, these missing qualities were supplanted by their normal of the things replied; those missing multiple things were viewed as absent. Cronbach's alpha in the 05 range extended from 0.87 to 0.90 (Malfa = .875).

3.2.5 FINAL RESULTS

Resources, SDs, and connections for the completed example appeared in Bench01; note that t-examinations were utilized to examine critical grouping contrasts at these methods, with the main contrasts being for the FS block and slant (p <.0001), as would be normal dependent on the gathering division portrayed by - down.

To measure the effect of vicissitudes in PS and F.S during money-related emergency before and after the period, we previously determined the intra-singular catching parameters (balance), direct changes over the retro (slant), and quadratics variation over the period (quadratics bend) for both PS and FS. This was done in a solitary model with the goal that the three parameters together completely mirror an individual's pressure or FS design; hence, these three parameters are constantly brought into the diagnostic models as a gathering and not independently. We utilized a similar technique to compute these parameters for the inherent individual balance, incline, and quadratic salary bend over the period as the best accessible controller for the impacts of target FS on every person. After the model arrangement was kept running on the filled example as a pattern, the example was partly founded on where individuals had a typical confident (>0) or adverse (<0) straight pattern in FS over time. Note that the intra-singular incline stricture utilized for this partition grouping is unique in relation to that utilized as an indicator in the breakdown; here, the direct slant of every individual is determined, overlooking the quadratic term, to give important slant estimates. All models anticipate wellbeing in wave 5 and incorporate a term controlling wellbeing toward the start. The example size is the equivalent for the figure models (full example = 311, adverse slant bunch = 155, confident incline bunch = 158) as the information was completed. Fundamental models inspected the immediate impacts and secondary impacts of every one of the statistic factors (age, sexual orientation, conjugal status, race, and training); as no noteworthy statistic contrasts rose, these rapports were excluded in the last replicas.

The first archetypal included 04 covariate terms: pattern wellbeing and individual counterbalance evaluations, slant, and quadratic pay bend. In the full example, in the two gatherings, more wellbeing side effects were estimated toward the start of information accumulation and essentially anticipated more wellbeing indications estimated toward the end of information gathering (p <.0001). None of the pay parameters fundamentally predicts tendency 05 wellbeing in the completed example or in the undesirable slant gathering, yet the quadratics salary tenure (quadrangle pay) is noteworthy in the optimistic incline gathering, for example, those with a progressively positive quadratic pattern in pay, which was a weakness (p = .02).

The Stress Model includes the three intra-singular stress intercepts (Tension Interrupt, Strain Slope, Strain Quadrangle), which enable us to examine the degree to which an individual's PS model predicts end-of-life wellbeing during the period, controlling the benchmark wellbeing. In the full example and in the negative incline gathering, each of the three pressure time frames are critical in the positive way, with the goal that you (a) have more prominent worry toward the start, (b) have a more noteworthy increment in worry over the period, and (c) the nearness of a progressively positive quadratic pressure bend over the period predicts weakening in wellbeing. Just the expression "stress capture" was important in the Optimistic Slope gathering.

The money-related study surveys the effect of FS during the review on wellbeing, in addition to the model the 03 intra-singular figures of FS (financial capture, financial incline, Finance Quad). Every one of the three terms anticipated wellbeing in the negative incline gathering, so the nearness of more awful FS at standard, the more noteworthy diminishing in FS during the review, and the nearness of an adverse quadratics bend in FS anticipated more terrible wellbeing. Conversely, nobody was an indicator in the Positive Slope gathering. In the completed example, just the impact of Financing Offset was critical.

The joined model incorporates both intra-singular PS terms and intra-singular FS terms. In the full example, stress impacts stay pertinent, yet budgetary block, which was significant previously, is never again critical. The joined archetypal in the productive tilt grouping expressions that when the 06 inside individual rapports are incorporated into the archetypal, the term for PS balance stays pertinent. The joined archetypal is the most enlightening in the adverse slant grouping, as both separate replicas (tension model and money-related archetypal) uncovered impacts of a moderately practically identical character, as demonstrated by the Archetypal R2 standards. The outcomes show that once every one of the 06 terms are incorporated into the model, the limits for changing the voltage (voltage slant, stress quadrature) stay pertinent, while the term for capturing the voltage ends up immaterial; such a model is seen under financing conditions, without any recuperations demonstrating any hugeness, yet the two impacts of evolving accounts (the incline of the funds and the money quadrature) hold their huge impacts.

3.2.6 Dialog

The outcomes mostly bolster the theories. To start with, in the general example, higher standard PS levels, lower gauge levels of apparent FS, and PS increments anticipate a decline in wellbeing toward the finish of the investigation time frame; be that as it may, the decrease in the apparent FS isn't. At the point when both pressure and money-related effects are viewed together, the impacts of PS are completely represented by the soundness of the first abstract FS. Given the gathering contrasts, the theorized model of results was found to a huge degree for the individuals who had a direct decrease in emotional FS over the period, with PS and FS limits consuming huge impacts. Though, the normal intervention impact is more fragile than anticipated, with the two variables keeping up noteworthy impacts in the consolidated model and proposing an increasingly added substance connection between the two. For the individuals who don't encounter the negative effect of the money-related emergency—the individuals who didn't have an adverse straight alteration in emotional FS over the review—the medical advantages theory isn't bolstered, since neither PS nor FS conditions anticipate wellbeing. Hence, it appears that a change in abstract FS influences wellbeing just in the event that it is negative and most likely reminiscent of stress.

Discoveries connecting more awful starting FS and declining FS with more unfortunate wellbeing results are likened with past work in the field demonstrating that pointers of monetary hardship and money-related pain foresee more terrible wellbeing (Davelos and Frinnch, 2010; Kahn and Pearlin, 2005; Lynich et al., 1998; Virtianen et al., 2001). The connection amid more elevated heights (or more prominent increments) of PS and less fortunate wellbeing likewise underpins past examinations where impressions of tension are solid indicators of corporeal wellbeing (Godboutis and Glaseir, 2005; Nielsen et al., 2007; Richardson et al., 2011), presumably According to the results and investigation showed in physical statistics weight it will intesect with the normal procetures and terminology of financail services completely (Juster et al., 2011; Merz et al., 2001). Since of the steady pressure wellbeing, it is unforeseen that the pressure parameters neglected to foresee the strength of persons in the productive-incline grouping; it might be that existence in this non-declining bunch throughout the overall downturn fills in as a checking or defensive issue in contradiction of these run-of-the-mill wellbeing impacts on pressure.

The unique purpose of this examination to this current work lies in the gathering investigation in which we contrast these impacts with those encountering an FS decrease during a time of monetary downturn with the individuals who don't. At the point when we take a look at this progressively explicit degree of investigation, we can see that the effect of changes in FS on wellbeing is shown distinctly for the individuals who feel the impacts of the financial downturn; that is, a more noteworthy decrease in FS during the downturn time frame predicts less fortunate wellbeing; however, a more noteworthy improvement in FS during the period doesn't foresee better wellbeing. This indicates that the pressure that goes with this money-related strain—and its impact on the physiological frameworks of the body—is a significant disruptor prompting antagonistic wellbeing impacts. The way that adjustments in PS and abstract FS anticipate wellbeing freely in this grouping of decreases demonstrates that strains coming about because of the apparent money-related downturn have negative wellbeing impacts over those by and large assessed by PS.

That every one of the "activities" in our studies happen with regard to the individuals who view themselves as encountering a decrease in FS during the downturn time frame takes us back to the apparent effect of these full-scale level logical occasions alone on conditions and working. Additionally stresses the apparent effect as a significant purpose of mediation to lighten the negative wellbeing impacts that so regularly go with times of monetary hardship. The idea of occasions at the full-scale level implies that we can't meddle with the source; in spite of the fact that it is perfect to prevent the procedure from the earliest starting point (monetary downturn → budgetary pressure/PS → wellbeing), as a rule it is basically unrealistic. Thus, as experts, we distinguish parts of individual recognition or ways to deal with these outer occasions and direct them for change and mediation. For instance, when seeing how individuals adapt to upsetting life conditions, such a change can be made either at the degree of appraisal (how we see and "size" a possibly compromising circumstance) or at the degree of adapting (how we submit assets, accessible to disperse mental and physiological enduring because of an undermining or testing circumstance; Lazarus and Folksman, 1982).

Comparing this to the current discoveries, an alternative to mitigate the apparent effect of the financial downturn and the subsequent worry at the valuation level is empowering individuals to objectively assess their spending limits, giving specific consideration to the amount they really have changed inside the most recent year (or since the start of the downturn). By advancing a progressively target appraisal of the genuine current money-related circumstance and by educating individuals how exciting media stories can impact their presumptions (Soroka, 2006), a portion of the pressure emerging from an undermining evaluation of the circumstance could disseminate and lessen long-term wellbeing impacts. Nonetheless, the individual effect of a large-scale financial occasion is probably going to be genuine; for this situation, changing the gauge is probably not going to be viable. Or maybe, the best purpose of intercession planned for diminishing the probability of negative wellbeing results would be at the degree of adapting. For instance, studies have discovered that reflection successfully lessens the negative effect of psychosocial stress, for example, monetary worry, on cardiovascular results (Walston et al., 2004); religion (Paragament, 1998) and communal help (Deliongis and Holtizman, 2004) are likewise compelling pressures that reduce overall tension (e.g., when the budget or money-related hardship can't be straightforwardly tended to). Despite the fact that this examination adds to existing writing from multiple points of view, there are impediments that should be recognized. To start with, the NDHWB isn't intended for the particular motivation behind testing these theories, and different measures might be progressively valuable in assessing these connections. For instance, wellbeing estimation has altered in wave 05 from the corporeal wellbeing estimation agenda (Belloc et al., 1970) to PIILL (Pennebaiker, 1981), which may affect the exactness of the examinations. As it is difficult to foresee the planning and particularity of these sorts of occasions at the large-scale level, and since the adjustment in the measure isn't mistaken for the outcomes, we accept that the information and examinations utilized here mirror an important window into the experience of GFCs in middle-aged and older adults. A subsequent restriction is that the procedures used to measure the key factors are emotional, which implies that a portion of the observed impacts could be because of a mutual strategy fluctuation. Albeit an endeavor is made to control progressively targeted FS data by consolidating intra-singular pay parameters into the model, the accessible pay data is less exact than would be hoped for. Third, we talk about the gathering contrasts that rose up out of the investigations, yet these distinctions were not expressly explored on account of the intricacy of the models; notwithstanding, we contend this is less risky when correlations are made among noteworthy and irrelevant impacts, as is done here.

Generally speaking, the discoveries underline that a large-scale level logical occasion can and does influence people in another way, with key components being the way these individuals see themselves to be influenced and the pressure that may come about because of feeling the intensity of these occasions. In spite of the fact that it isn't constantly conceivable to focus on the occasion itself, a portion of the unfriendly impacts of such occasions on wellbeing and prosperity can be relieved by adjusting levels of apparent effect or stress across the board.

REFERENCES

Belloc, N. B., Breslow, L., & Hochstim, J. R. (1971). Measurement of physical health in a general population survey. *American journal of epidemiology*, *93*(5), 328–336.

Bronfenbrenner, U. (1977). Toward an experimental ecology of human development. *American psychologist*, *32*(7), 513.

Bronfenbrenner, U. & Ceci, S. J. (1994). Nature-nuture reconceptualized in developmental perspective: A bio ecological model. *Psychological review*, *101*(4), 568.

Cohen, S., Kamarck, T., & Mermelstein, R. (1983). A global measure of perceived stress. *Journal of health and social behavior*, 385–396.

French, M. T., & Davalos, M. E. (2011). This recession is wearing me out! Health-related quality of life and economic downturns. *Journal of Mental Health Policy and Economics*, *14*(2), 61–72.

Godbout, J. P., & Glaser, R. (2006). Stress-induced immune dysregulation: implications for wound healing, infectious disease and cancer. *Journal of Neuroimmune Pharmacology*, *1*(4), 421–427.

Juster, R. P., McEwen, B. S., & Lupien, S. J. (2010). Allostatic load biomarkers of chronic stress and impact on health and cognition. *Neuroscience & Biobehavioral Reviews*, *35*(1), 2–16.

Kahn, J. R., & Pearlin, L. I. (2006). Financial strain over the life course and health among older adults. *Journal of health and social behavior*, *47*(1), 17–31.

Kulkarni, M. (2013). Social determinants of health: The role of neighbourhoods, psychological factors and health behaviours in predicting health outcomes for the urban poor in India. *Journal of health psychology*, *18*(1), 96–109.

Lazarus, R. S., & Folkman, S. (1984). *Stress, appraisal, and coping*. Springer publishing company.

Lynch, J. W., Kaplan, G. A., & Shema, S. J. (1997). Cumulative impact of sustained economic hardship on physical, cognitive, psychological, and social functioning. *New England Journal of Medicine*, *337*(26), 1889–1895.

Merz, C. N. B., Dwyer, J., Nordstrom, C. K., Walton, K. G., Salerno, J. W., & Schneider, R. H. (2002). Psychosocial stress and cardiovascular disease: pathophysiological links. *Behavioral Medicine*, *27*(4), 141–147.

Neumayer, E. (2004). Recessions lower (some) mortality rates: evidence from Germany. *Social science & medicine*, *58*(6), 1037–1047.

Nielson, N. R., Kristensen, T. S., Schnohr, P., & Gronbaek, M. (2008). Perceived stress and cause-specific mortality among men and women: Results from a prospective study. *American Journal of Epidemiology, 168*(5), 481–491.

Regidor, E., Barrio, G., Bravo, M. J., & de la Fuente, L. (2014). Has health in Spain been declining since the economic crisis? *J Epidemiol Community Health, 68*(3), 280–282.

Richardson, S., Shaffer, J. A., Falzon, L., Krupka, D., Davidson, K. W., & Edmondson, D. (2012). Meta-analysis of perceived stress and its association with incident coronary heart disease. *The American journal of cardiology, 110*(12), 1711–1716.

Soroka, S. N. (2006). Good news and bad news: Asymmetric responses to economic information. *The journal of Politics, 68*(2), 372–385.

Virtanen, M., Kivimäki, M., Joensuu, M., Virtanen, P., Elovainio, M., & Vahtera, J. (2005). Temporary employment and health: a review. *International journal of epidemiology, 34*(3), 610–622.

4 Comparative Study of Memory Architectures for Multiprocessor Systems-on-Chip (MPSoC)

Kaoutar Aamali, Abdelhakim Alali,
Mohamed Sadik, and Zineb El Hariti
Hassan II University of Casablanca,
Casablanca, Morocco

CONTENTS

4.1 INTRODUCTION

The majority of current applications are complex and need a high-performance multiprocessor. The design stages of each System-on-Chip and integrated circuits, in general, go through various levels of abstraction.

The complexity of systems continues to increase; thus, studying the tools and techniques of silicon allows for fast progress for the fabrication of transistors; modeling these systems at a better level of abstraction at the beginning of their design reduces complexity in terms of development and offers the developer the possibility and the advantages of simulating the system at an early stage to make a performance estimate [1].

The optimization from the memory architecture of these systems has found an interest in industrial and academic research because of its role of improving the

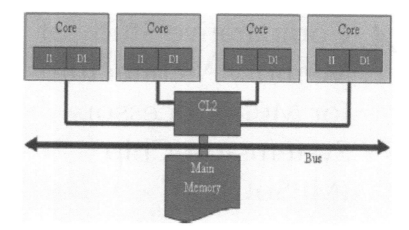

FIGURE 4.1   Quad-core architecture INTEL.

performance of MPSoCs, such as speed and energy consumption [2], using high-level models that allow for estimation of temperature and power.

In the embedded systems, researchers are concentrating on developing architecture memory and [3] hierarchy of the cache memory. A. Asaduzzaman et al [4] show that more cache misses mean a decrease in performance. However, even if the architecture with cache memory shows an improvement in the performance of the systems, on the other hand, the system consumes more power [5].

The architecture of the INTEL multiprocessor shown in Figure 4.1 has a shared memory, as the cores have a distributed memory architecture. On the other hand, the AMD processor shown in Figure 4.2 offers another solution, opting for a shard cache memory at level3.

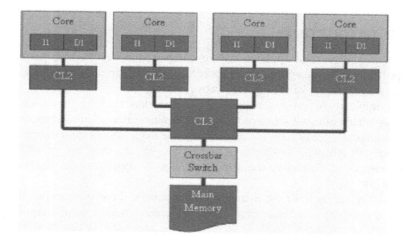

FIGURE 4.2   Quad-core architecture AMD.

The main objective of this study is to design a new memory architecture for the LIBTLMPWT open-source platform [6] that allows one to compare several software programs in terms of architecture to simulate the behavior of the energy consumed and the temperature generated by each component of the chip while using a high level of abstraction.

The rest of the chapter is organized as follows. Section 4.2 presents an overview of the related works in memory architecture. Section 4.3, exhibits the results obtained by comparing the different memory architecture in terms of performance and discuss these results. Finally, section 4.4 concludes the paper.

4.2 COMPARATIVE SURVEY

4.2.1 SHARED MEMORY SYSTEMS

The majority of existing multicore software opts for the use of a shared memory architecture, as shown in Figure 4.3, in which a block of memory is shared by all processors. E.Viaud et al [7] propose a method to minimize the simulation time based on the new theory of parallel discrete events (PDEs) while using a shared memory architecture, in which the shared memory bank can integrate the code and the data, respectively.

The same memory architecture was presented by D. Kim et al and S. Boukhechem [8, 9], who validated a new technique for co-simulation hardware and software at a high level of abstraction for heterogeneous MPSoCs platforms. A. Rahimi et al [10] used a synthesizable logarithmic that connects with each other—in other words, it allows several processor cores to be connected along a multibanked, tightly coupled single data storage location.

M. R. Kakoee et al [11] have used the logarithmic interconnect network proposed by [10] with an addition of a shared data cache memory L1, this has been compared with a Tightly Coupled Data Memory architecture (TCDM). The results show that the

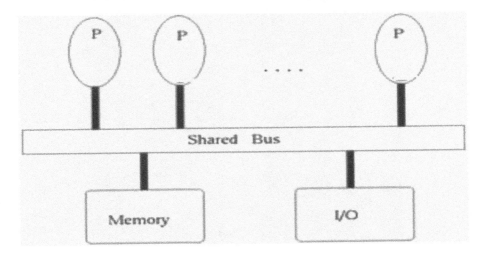

FIGURE 4.3 Shared memory architecture.

use of shared-L1 cache indicated that the area is lower than 18% compared to TCDM for the case of a cluster in which we can find 16 processors and 32 cached memory and shows overhead varies between (5% to 30%) depending on the processor size.

However, these systems offer a programing design that allows for rapid data sharing via a uniform action for reading and writing shared organization in the global memory. This model is also retained by J. Tendler et al, L. Hammond et al, and R. B. Atitallah et al [12–14].

The ease and portability of programing on such systems significantly reduce the cost of developing parallel applications. On the other hand, these systems suffer from a great latency in memory access, which limits their flexibility.

4.2.2 DISTRIBUTED SHARED MEMORY SYSTEMS

This is a relatively new concept that combines a shared memory architecture and distributed memory architecture. The distributed memory architecture shown in Figure 4.4 illustrates how the memory is distributed among all the processors. The systems of Freescale and S. Han et al [15, 16] use this process, which has access to write data, but the communication between the processors in the case of data sharing degrades system performance, and that makes this architecture little considered in industrial and academic research.

The distributed shared memory programing is an interesting problem for M. Monchiero et al [17]. They try to exploit this architecture by focusing on the amelioration of the latency and the energy of the system. J. Zhang et al [18], proposed

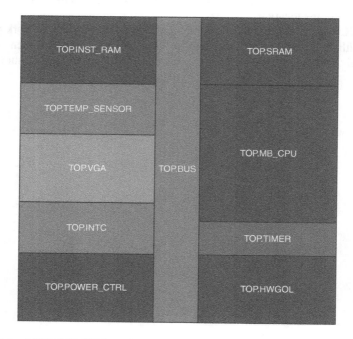

FIGURE 4.4   LIBTLMPWT floorplan.

an experiment on a Multi-core NOC platform with a distributed shared memory architecture (DSM) managed by the Data Management Engine (DME). Whereas the comparison based on a centralized memory architecture, the implementation of these platforms on an Altera Stratix IV FPGA, with an H.264 decoder, clearly showed an improvement in the performance carried by the distributed shared memory architecture (DSM). However, Z. Yuang [19] has proposed a scalable distributed memory architecture, insofar as access to memory must be organized and structured, the simulations of this architecture with a Network on Chip responded to the problem of high parallelism and the results confirm a flexible programing mode. P. Francesco et al [20] proposed a reliable hardware/software support for communication with the use of message passing and understood the process of sending simple messages on a DSM architecture. However, the DSM systems keep the ease of the programing of shared memory systems by preserving flexibility and speed.

4.3   DISCUSSION OF PERFORMANCE COMPARISONS

In this section, we conduct performance comparisons between systems with a shared memory architecture and DSM .The comparison is shown in Table 4.1, as proposed by R. Garibotti et al [21]. They show a reduction of up to 50% in the energy dissipation specified in the DSM compared to centralized shared memory (CSM). On the other hand, the results prove an improvement of ×3 in the speed of the DSM compared to CSM.

J. Ax et al [22] prove that latency will improve by using a DSM. The results of J. Zhang et al [18] which executed the decoder H.264 on 6-nodes and 9-nodes with two types of images, CIF and QCIF, are shown in Table 4.2, and it clearly shows that the DSM has improved performance by 1 to 2 times.

TABLE 4.1
Energy Dissipation Comparison: DSM vs. CSM

Cache Memory Sizes	DSM	CSM
2KB	8 uJ	15 uJ
4KB	7 uJ	5 uJ

TABLE 4.2
Performance Comparison: DSM vs. CSM

Node	CSM	DSM
6	26 fps	50 fps
9	27 fps	75 fps

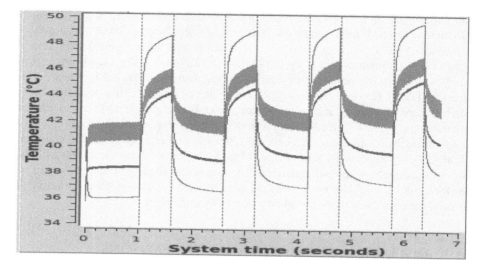

FIGURE 4.5   Temperature plots for the "game of life."

This study clearly shows the advantage of DSM architecture that will be used to optimize the performance of the LIBTLMPWT platform.

In the platform, the calculations are integrated into the SystemC/TLM model, with each module counting the algorithm to estimate energy, the collection of information using tool analytical temperature for multiprocessors (ATMI) [23]. The platform also has a graphical user interface, as shown in Figures 4.4 and 4.5, providing implementation of simulation controls using the QT framework.

4.4   CONCLUSION

This chapter proposes a literature study on the different memory architectures of multiprocessor systems on a chip, since the model of DSM shows a very high performance. In future work, we would develop an architecture model of a multiprocessor system on a chip with DSM at a high level of abstraction.

REFERENCES

[1] A. Alali, I. Assayad, and M. Sadik, "Modeling and simulation of multiprocessor systems MPSoC by SystemC/TLM2", International Journal of Computer Science Issues (IJCSI), 11(3), 103, 2014.
[2] Z. El Hariti, A. Alali, and M. Sadik, "Power and temperature estimation for soft-core processor task at the SystemC/TLM", In 2018 6th International Conference on Multimedia Computing and Systems (ICMCS), IEEE, pp. 1–5, May 2018.

[3] I. Loi, and L. Benini, "A multi banked—multi ported—non blocking shared L2 cache for MPSoC platforms", In 2014 Design, Automation & Test in Europe Conference & Exhibition (DATE), IEEE, pp. 1–6, March 2014.

[4] A. Asaduzzaman, F. N. Sibai, and M. Rani, "Impact of level-2 cache sharing on the performance and power requirements of homogeneous multicore embedded systems", Microprocessors and Microsystems, 33(5–6), 388–397, 2009.

[5] D. Lenoski, J. Laudon, K. Gharachorloo, W. D. Weber, A. Gupta, J. Hennessy, and M. S. Lam, "The Stanford dash multiprocessor", Computer, 25(3), 63–79, 1992.

[6] M. Moy, C. Helmstetter, T. Bouhadiba, and F. Maraninchi, "Modeling power consumption and temperature in TLM models", 3(1), 1–29, 2016.

[7] E. Viaud, F. Pêcheux, and A. Greiner, "An efficient TLM/T modeling and simulation environment based on conservative parallel discrete event principles", In Proceedings of the Design Automation & Test in Europe Conference, IEEE, Vol. 1, pp. 1–6, March 2006.

[8] D. Kim, Y. Yi, and S. Ha, "Trace-driven HW/SW cosimulation using virtual synchronization technique", In Proceedings of 42nd Design Automation Conference, IEEE, pp. 345–348, June 2005.

[9] S. Boukhechem, "Contribution à la mise en place d'une plateforme open-source MPSoC sous SystemC pour la Co-simulation d'architectures hétérogènes (Doctoral dissertation, Dijon)", 2008.

[10] A. Rahimi, I. Loi, M. R. Kakoee, and L. Benini, "A fully-synthesizable single-cycle interconnection network for shared-L1 processor clusters", In 2011 Design, Automation & Test in Europe, IEEE, pp. 1–6, March 2011.

[11] M. R. Kakoee, V. Petrovic, and L. Benini, "A multi-banked shared-L1 cache architecture for tightly coupled processor clusters", In 2012 International Symposium on System on Chip (SoC), IEEE, pp. 1–5, October 2012.

[12] J. M. Tendler, J. S. Dodson, J. S. Fields, H. Le, and B. Sinharoy, "POWER4 system microarchitecture", IBM Journal of Research and Development, 46(1), 5–25, 2002.

[13] L. Hammond, B. A. Hubbert, M. Siu, M. K. Prabhu, M. Chen, and K. Olukolun, "The stanford hydra CMP", IEEE Micro, 20(2), 71–84, 2000.

[14] R. B. Atitallah, S. Niar, and J. L. Dekeyser, "MPSoC power estimation framework at transaction level modeling", In 2007 International Conference on Microelectronics, IEEE, pp. 245–248, December 2007.

[15] F. Semiconductor, MPC8641D Integrated Host Processor Family Reference Manual. July 2008. http://www. freescale.com

[16] S. I. Han, A. Baghdadi, M. Bonaciu, S. I. Chae, and A. A. Jerraya, "An efficient scalable and flexible data transfer architecture for multiprocessor SoC with massive distributed memory", In Proceedings of the 41st Annual Design Automation Conference, pp. 250–255, June 2004.

[17] M. Monchiero, G. Palermo, C. Silvano, and O. Villa, "Exploration of distributed shared memory architectures for NoC-based multiprocessors", Journal of Systems Architecture, 53(10), 719–732, 2007.

[18] J. Zhang, Z. Yu, Z. Yu, K. Zhang, Z. Lu, and A. Jantsch, "Efficient distributed memory management in a multi-core H. 264 decoder on FPGA", In 2013 International Symposium on System on Chip (SoC), IEEE, pp. 1–4, October 2013.

[19] Z. Yuang, L. Li, Y. Shengguang, D. Lan, L. Xiaoxiang, and G. Minglun, "A scalable distributed memory architecture for Network on Chip", In APCCAS 2008-2008 IEEE Asia Pacific Conference on Circuits and Systems, IEEE, pp. 1260–1263, November 2008.

[20] P. Francesco, P. Antonio, and P. Marchal, "Flexible hardware/software support for message passing on a distributed shared memory architecture", In Design, Automation and Test in Europe, IEEE, pp. 736–741, March 2005.

[21] R. Garibotti, A. Butko, L. Ost, A. Gamatié, G. Sassatelli, and C. Adeniyi-Jones, "Efficient embedded software migration towards clusterized distributed-memory architectures", IEEE Transactions on Computers, 65(8), 2645–2651, 2015.

[22] J. Ax, G. Sievers, J. Daberkow, M. Flasskamp, M. Vohrmann, T. Jungeblut, and U. Rückert, "CoreVA-MPSoC: A many-core architecture with tightly coupled shared and local data memories", IEEE Transactions on Parallel and Distributed Systems, 29(5), 1030–1043, 2018.

[23] P. Michaud, and Y. Sazeides, "ATMI: Analytical model of temperature in microprocessors", In Third Annual Workshop on Modeling, Benchmarking and Simulation (MoBS), Vol. 2, p. 7, June 2007.

5 Assessment of Heating and Cooling Energy Needs in Residential Buildings in Settat, Morocco

Abdellah Boussafi and Najat Ouaaline
Hassan 1st University, Settat, Morocco

CONTENTS

5.1 INTRODUCTION

Energy has become indispensable for both human and economic development of society. After the first oil shock, fossil energy deposits have become scarce and the cost of energy is increasing. However, climate and environmental upheavals are the main factors leading to an awareness of the rational use of energy.

Buildings are at the heart of the energy issue, which represents about half of the total energy consumption of Morocco. All the parts of a building are subject to heat transfer, and a good control of the latter leads to good management of energy consumption.

Our work in this case is to evaluate the energy needs in the heating and cooling of a residential apartment building located in Settat in the Chaouia region in Morocco.

In order to carry out this evaluation, our work will carry out the following plan:

- In the first part, we model our building as the subject of the study.
- The second part will be reserved for the results and the discussion.

5.2   MODELING THE BUILDING

5.2.1   Building

The residential building chosen for our study is an apartment with a living area of 110 m² with an overall floor-to-ceiling ratio of 17.5%.

$$TGBV = \frac{\sum \text{Surfaces of windows of external walls}}{\sum \text{Gross surfaces of exterior walls}} \tag{5.1}$$

5.2.2   Meteorological Data

It is necessary to introduce weather data collected from the Meteonorm software in order to carry out the dynamic thermal simulations with the TRNsys software.

Thus, the Kingdom of Morocco is divided into six climatic zones according to the criteria of temperature, humidity, and direct and diffuse horizontal radiation (Figure 5.1).

In our study, we took Settat as a representative city for zone 1, where our building is located. Table 5.1 presents these geographic coordinates.

5.2.3   Hypothesis of Dynamic Thermal Simulation

5.2.3.1   Contributions Due to Occupants

The human body is assimilated as much as a thermal system whose power depends on the activity exerted. In our study, the apartment studied is occupied by a young couple, and Table 5.2 describes the occupancy benefit of this building.

The TRNsys software represents a set of several types of occupant gains based on the 7730 standard. For our case, we have the following:

- **Kitchen:** 185W/Person
- **Living room:** 170W/Person
- **Other rooms:** 100W/Person

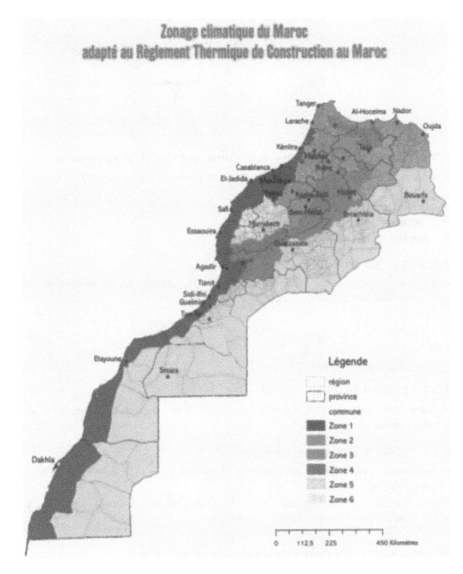

FIGURE 5.1   Morocco's climate zonation.

TABLE 5.1
Geographic Coordinates of Settat

Area	City	Altitude	Longitude	Latitude
Area 1	Settat	365 m	−7,6160	33,0010

TABLE 5.2
Building Occupancy Benefit

Time	Occupation
Week (17:00–08:00)	2
Weekend	2

5.2.3.2 The Contributions Due to Lighting and Electrical Appliances

The electrical usage of lighting and electrical appliances are as follows:

- **Computers:** 230W/PC
- **Lighting:** 10W/m²
- **Appliances:** 4500W

5.2.3.3 The Air Change Rate

The air renewal rate, or the brewing rate, is fixed according to the Moroccan standard 13789/2010 at 0.6 vol/h.

$$ACH = \frac{\text{Blown air flow (m}^3.\text{h)}}{\text{Volume of the room(m}^3)} \tag{5.2}$$

5.2.3.4 Internal Shading

The value of the internal shading is fixed at 25% of the surface of the exterior windows throughout the year.

5.2.3.5 Heating and Air Conditioning

The installed air conditioning system allows stabilizing the temperature at 25°C and the heating maintenance at 20°C.

So we divided our building into three zones based on temperature, direction, and profiles of occupants (Figure 5.2).

5.3 RESULTS AND DISCUSSION

Various simulations have been carried out on the studied building, following baseline scenarios that involve considering the building constructed without any measure of energy efficiency.

Figure 5.3 describes our simulation model with the TRNsys software environment.

The graph of Figure 5.4 shows the electrical energy consumption in the case of the building with a heating and cooling system (the blue graph) and without them (the black graph).

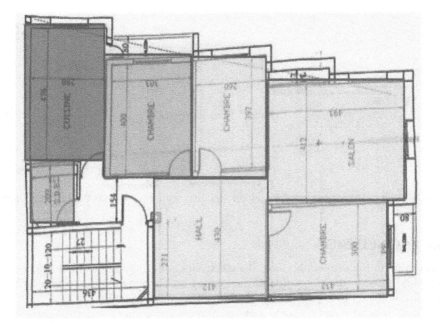

FIGURE 5.2   Thermal zoning of the habitat.

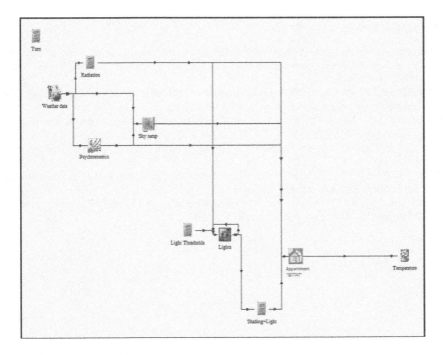

FIGURE 5.3   Project with TRNsys.

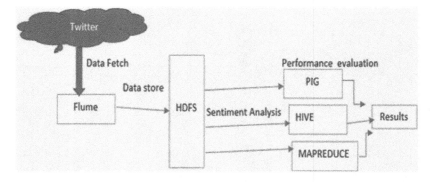

FIGURE 5.4 Annual consumption of the building with and without the heating/cooling system.

5.4 CONCLUSION

According to the results obtained, the electricity consumption has increased twice, and this is due to the adaptation of the heating and cooling system, which exceeds the thresholds set by the Moroccan Building Thermal Regulation.

These lead us to a thorough study on the optimization of natural lighting and design to prevent the energy loss and improve airtightness and ensure high thermal inertia.

BIBLIOGRAPHY

S. Ferrari and V. Zanotto, 2016. Building Energy Performance Assessment in Southern Europe, PoliMISpringerBriefs, Réglementation thermique de construction au Maroc "RTCM". AMEE.

N. Morel et E. Gnansounou, 2007. Énergétique du bâtiment. https://docplayer.fr/20497150-Energetique-du-batiment.html (accessed May 2021).

R. Kharchi, 2013. Etude Energétique de chauffage, rafraichissement et eau sanitaire d'une maison type en Algérie.

G. Krauss, B. Lips, J. Virgone, E. Blanco, 2006. Modélisation sous TRNSys d'une maison à énergie positive.

Règles Th-Bat, 2015. https://www.ademe.fr/sites/default/files/assets/documents/th-bat-publication-2015.pdf (accessed May 2021).

Manuel du logiciel TRNSys 16. http://web.mit.edu/parmstr/Public/Documentation/05-MathematicalReference.pdf (accessed May 2021).

6 Authentication Model Using the JADE Framework for Communication Security in Multiagent Systems

Sanae Hanaoui, Jalal Laassiri, and Yousra Berguig
Ibn Tofail University, Kenitra, Morocco

CONTENTS

6.1 INTRODUCTION

Guaranteeing the security of communication is the number one addressed issue in all systems, which relies on the authentication procedure. The authentication procedure is a process for identifying and verifying the identity of the questioned subject [2, 3]. In case the authentication process fails, the authenticated part will not be able to perform any operation for which it was accorded permission. The agent technology has imposed itself in the field of computer science and gained acceptance; however, the agent security is still a challenge that has not obtained enough attention from the agent community [4]. Nevertheless, with the aim of using a mobile agent in e-commerce solutions to provide unrestricted secure solutions and efficiency, the agent security that is lacking has to be addressed. In this paper, we are concerned with the security of multiagent authentication, especially via authentication with the protocols SSL and TLS and by adopting other cryptographical techniques into the developed solution.

Mobile agents may engage in variant multiagent system (MAS) platform providers. With the intent of protecting both the agent owner platform and the receiver platform, it is an obligation to assure their integrity, as well as the level of trust in the migration process [5, 6]. As we consider the security requirements for MAS, authentication is an important required state between the communicated platforms; that is, both platforms (the sender host and the receiver host) must authenticate each other. MAS authentication refers to a process in which the platform ensures that the other platform in the communication is the one who it is declared to be [7]. In this work, we aim to secure the authentication of the mobile agent for the main platform in communication.

The remainder of this paper is organized as follows. Section 2 briefly investigates the security problems in MAS and exposes various communication threats on mobile agents and explores some security requirements to protect it. In Section 3, we will discuss the protocols SSL and TLS and our motivation for choosing these protocols. Section 4 elaborates on some of the backgrounds of research. Section 5 gives detailed information about the authentication approach adopted to secure our agent. In Section 6, we elaborate on the implementation of the approach. Finally, Section 7 concludes the paper.

6.1.1 Mobile Agent Security Countermeasures

The mobile agent faces critical security risks because of its strong mobility where its code, data, and state are exposed to other platforms into which it migrates for getting information or execution in the sake of accomplishing a designated goal. It gives either a malicious platform or another agent a chance to alter or even kill the agent before it attains its goal or accomplishes its assigned task. Therefore, the following security properties should be taken into consideration [8–10] so that the agent will be more certain about the visited platform and vice versa:

- Authentication and authorization: By assuring that communication initiates from its originator.
- Privacy and confidentiality: Assuring confidentiality of exchanges and interactions in an MAS in order to secure the communication of a mobile agent with its environment.
- Nonrepudiation: By logging important communication exchanges to prevent later denials.
- Accountability: By recording not only unique identification and authentication but also an audit log of security-relevant events, which means all security-related activities must be recorded for auditing and tracking purposes.

In addition, audit logs must be protected from unauthorized access and modifications.

- Availability: The agent platform should be capable of detecting and recovering from software and hardware failures. It should be able to deal with DoS attacks and to prevent them as well.
- Anonymity: The mother platform should keep the agent's identity hidden from other agents and maintain anonymity and determine the identity when necessary and legal.
- Fairness or trust: The necessity to ensure fair agent platform interaction where the agent should be able to assess the trustworthiness of information received from another agent or from an agent platform.

6.1.2   SSL/TLS DISCUSSION

SSL and TLS are the most advised and widely used secure communication protocols to create a secure link between a server and a client machine over the Internet [11, 12].

6.1.2.1   Secure Sockets Layer Protocol

This is a security protocol that is used to encrypt connections between two parties [13], most commonly between a web browser and a web server. This is commonly referred to by the dual moniker SSL/TLS, since the protocol suite was upgraded and renamed TLS in 1999. The intent of SSL was to provide secure communication using classical TCP sockets with few changes in application programming interface (API) usage of sockets to be able to leverage security on existing TCP socket code. The SSL/TSL protocol empowers the security of web applications or any other kind of application as underlying infrastructural components. As a separate protocol, it is inserted between the application protocol (HTTP) and the transport protocol (TCP) [14].

6.1.2.2   Motivation

We opted for SSL/TLS because it provides authentication (signature authentication), confidentiality, and integrity. However, TLS provides a more secure method for managing authentication and exchanging messages [15, 16], and because the authentication of the agent is less developed by the JADE community. However, the JADE-S platform requires that users (the owner of the agent or the container) must be authenticated by providing a username and password in order to be able to perform instructions on the platform. However, it doesn't authenticate a mobile agent itself so that the visited platform verifies the identity of the arrived agent to ensure that the agent has not become malicious as a consequence of alterations to its state.

6.2   RELATED WORKS

The research in the area of mobile agent development and applicability is still active, especially in terms of the security of this technology. Several projects have developed execution environments for mobile agents. However, authentication mechanisms have been partially discussed and addressed:

Vila, Schuster, and Riera [17] have explored the challenges, issues, and solutions to fulfil the security requirements of an MAS based on the JADE framework. By presenting a sufficient security vision for MAS, several security features are considered, from the authentication over encryption of the exchanged data up to the authorization of the access to services assigned only to a determined group. In the same sense, Bayer and Reich [5] have addressed specific security requirements for mobile software agents; one of these requirements is the authentication and possible threats for agent system operations in the context of Java Agent Development; their main objective was to show existing vulnerabilities and security breaches by analyzing the security of the JADE platform, giving existing improvements to the confidentiality of software agents merging from one agent platform to another and introducing trusted agents and their implementation in JADE. Berkovits, Guttman, and Swarup [18] have granted three security goals for mobile agent systems and have proposed an abstract architecture to achieve those goals. Their architecture is based on four distinct trust relationships between the principles of mobile agent systems. They have used existing theory—the distributed authentication theory of Lampson et al.—to clarify the architecture and to show that it meets its objectives. Ismail and Emirates [19] have described authentication mechanisms for mobile agents. In these mechanisms, the authentication of mobile agents is controlled by the mobile agent platforms using a digital signature and a public key infrastructure. Agents are authenticated via the authentication of their running platforms.

6.3   PROPOSED APPROACH

The authentication approach that we propose is based on signature authentication, where signature authentication is an alternative method of identifying who you are to a server, instead of typing the password. In our case, it is to identify multiagent authentication to the visited platform or server using the signature authentication, as well by authenticating the agent platform and the intended visited platform using the protocol SSL/TLS. Therefore, we propose that both the platform and agent identify each other on arrival to the destination platform by requesting authentication using the protocol TLS, which is valid for multiple user authentication–based agent servers (Figure 6.1).

6.3.1   DESCRIPTION OF THE APPROACH

Our approach is designated to respect the presented scenario in the Architectural Overview section. When a mobile agent calls the migration method the hosted platform, as we have detailed in our paper [20], it encrypts a formatted header using the RSA algorithm that consists of the agent owner identifier, the agent's code permission, and the agent's unique identifier, in addition to a signature of data or code, after generating the agent code and state signature using a private key. The agent (state and code) along with its header is sent to the destination server. On reception of the signed agent associated with its identifier header, the receiving server requests a TLS authentication to authenticate the mobile agent platform that sends the agent. In case of multiple migrations, the master agent invokes a signing agent, which will be in charge of signing, verifying, and validating the agent authentication. In the

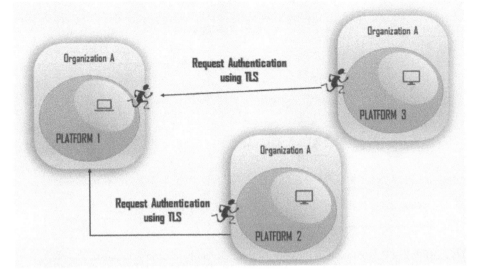

FIGURE 6.1 Authentication process.

case of a multi-authentication request, the agent's platform invokes in parallel the adequate number of processing agents. Each agent will be in charge of receiving the authentication request and validating the certificate by communicating the keys to the invoker of the TLS authentication in order to validate the sent signatures. Then, the receiving server decides whether to accept or reject the execution of the agent based on the successful authentication and digital certification verification of the agent platform after the communication of the session keys (Figure 6.2).

6.3.2 EXPERIMENTATION: IMPLEMENTATION ON JADE

In the present section, we present an architectural overview of the proposed mobile agent scenario followed by a description of our implementation of the authentication approach. This implementation is conducted in the JADE platform, and we are limiting our simulation on containers located in the same physical platform. The practical tests of the implementation are carried out in a machine which contains two containers that will represent the destination machines and the main container for the hosted agent. For the creation, management, mobility, and execution of agents, we adopt the JADE Snapshot during the agent trip from the native platform to the hosting platform.

6.3.2.1 Architectural Overview

Each agent platform or server in the system communicates with a trusted third-party certification authority (CA) to obtain a private key and its corresponding digital certificate. The agent server's digital certificate is digitally signed by the CA. A KeyStore is associated with each agent platform or server in the system, which is used to store and manage private keys along with their corresponding digital certificates.

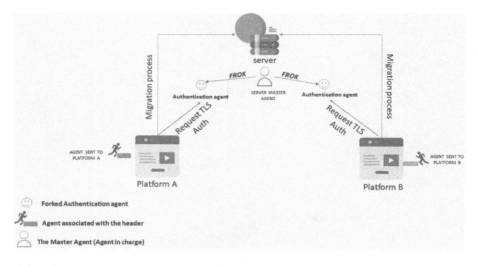

FIGURE 6.2   The scenario of the approach for two authentications requests.

The hosted platform or agent server retrieves its private key and the corresponding digital certificate from the KeyStore to sign a mobile agent and its header. The signed mobile agent associated with its header is then sent to the destination platform. On reception of the mobile agent associated with its header, the visited platform initiates a TLS connection to retrieve the CA's digital signature and to decrypt the mobile agent's header and to verify the agent signature in order to make sure that the right agent does the right thing.

To summarize the design of our minimal implementation for a secure mobile agent authentication, an agent migration to a destination agent server consists of the following steps (Figures 6.3 and 6.4):

a. Serialization of the state of the assigned agent.
b. Serialization of the state of the agent and associating the agent with the header.
c. Retrieval of the agent platform private key and digital certificate from the local KeyStore.
d. Creation of an object signature to be used in signing the agent.
e. Initialization of the signature object with the server private key.
f. Updating the signature object using the agent's state for encoding.
g. Generation of the mobile agent signature using the signature object from step (d).
h. Generation of our agent header and then encrypting our header using the private key which includes the signature and sender agent.
i. Associating the header to agent's state, code and sending of the agent header and the agent to the destination agent server.
j. Reception of the agent in the destination agent server or platform and creation of a new thread for the execution of the agent.

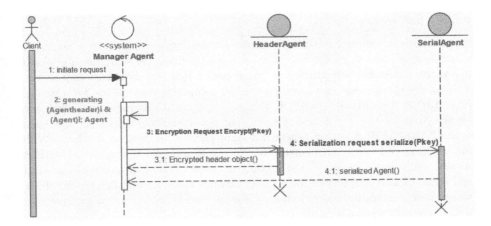

FIGURE 6.3   Authentication scenario hosted platform.

k. Initiating the communication using the TLS protocol for retrieval of the sender agent server's public key and digital certificate.

l. Deserialization of the agent's state.

m. Decrypt the header using the CA's public key shared by the protocol TLS after verification of the sender agent server's digital certificate using the CA's public key from step (k).

n. Verification of the agent's signature.

o. Run the agent if verification succeeds.

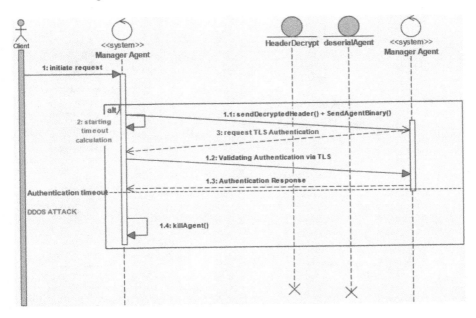

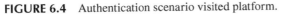

FIGURE 6.4   Authentication scenario visited platform.

6.3.3 SIMULATION

We will adopt a concrete illustration for the authentication scenario by considering a mobile agent that visits the web sites of several pharmacies searching for a plan that meets a customer's requirements. We focus on four servers: a customer server, a pharmacy's server, and two servers owned by competing pharmacies, for instance, FARMACIE A and FARMACIE B. The mobile agent is programed by a web site for selecting the best prepharmacy price. The agent Manager dispatches the agent to the FARMACIE A server, where the agent queries the product database. With the results stored in its environment, then the agent migrates to the FARMACIE B server, where again it queries the product database. The agent compares product and price information, decides on a plan, migrates to the appropriate prepharmacy server, and reserves the desired product. Finally, the agent returns to the customer with the results (Figure 6.5).

6.3.4 TEST

This part of the section presents the execution time of the proposed solution using the JADE platform. We are limiting our simulation to containers located in the same physical platform as a distributed architecture (Figure 6.5) using the presented resources at the beginning of the section. We intend to develop this solution to a distributed one.

For the creation, management, mobility, and execution of agents, we adopted JADE Snapshot. During the trip of the agent from the native platform to the visiting platforms, it performed many operations to ensure the proposed approach. From the results, it is observed that for communicating the public key between the agent platform and the visited platform it took less than 140 ms. By using the TLS protocol, as for encrypting

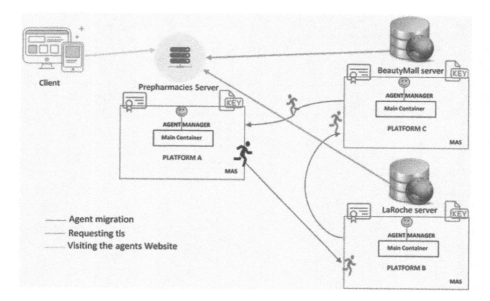

FIGURE 6.5   Simulation architecture in the JADE platform.

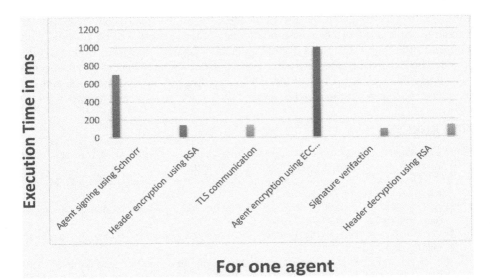

For one agent

FIGURE 6.6 Execution time for one agent.

the header using RSA, which contains information that verifies the agents, it has taken almost 173 ms., while by using Schnorr signature to ensure the integrity of our data, it has taken less than 700 ms., and for the ECC elliptic curve, it has taken 1200 ms. to encrypt our agent and guarantee its confidentiality. It has taken almost 10 ms. for the migration time of the agent associated with its header for each container. As for the decryption of the header agent at its arrival to its destination container, it is similar to the encryption time, while for the signature verification it has taken less than 100 ms. Given the use of a distributed platform in a single machine, we might conclude the total execution time has a value of 2323 ms., which is very promising for the use of the proposed approach in securing web application while considering the security of the agent itself both for the visited and the main platform (Figure 6.6).

6.4 CONCLUSION

In this work, we explored some security requirements for mobile agents and presented the most used secure communication protocol, SSL/TLS, and we also gave our motivation for using this protocol in our authentication approach in order to secure the agent authentication. The presented approach is based on digital signatures and public key infrastructure shared with the TLS communication protocol. In this model, we expected that agents would come from a trusted platform and that the hosted platform agent would be assured about the other agents, since the visited platform which executes an agent has partial and sometimes full control over that agent. In addition, the proposed authentication approach is adequate for any MAS platform, or a trusted server that is able to run the agents. Due to digitally signing the agent every time it is sent, we grant both its nonrepudiation and integrity; thus, it is easy to identify a malicious platform sending a malicious agent. The agent platform from which we receive an agent has to verify the integrity of the agent from the previous sender by verifying the associated header to the arrived agent. In case of alteration, the signature will be nonvalid. Our authentication approach ensures that the visited mobile agent was not altered in its way, and therefore the visited platform can be sure that there were no changes in the agent's state, and it can execute its instruction safely accordingly to the code permission in the associated header of the agent which authenticates both the agent and its owner.

REFERENCES

[1] L. C. Paulson, "Inductive analysis of the internet protocol TLS." ACM Transactions on Information and System Security, vol. 2, no. 3, 1999.

[2] W. Goralski, "Securing sockets with SSL," in The Illustrated Network, Morgan Kaufmann, 2009, pp. 585–606.

[3] N. Constantinescu and C. I. Popirlan, Authentication model based on multi-agent system, vol. 38, no. 2, pp. 59–68, 2011.

[4] G. Stoneburner, Underlying Technical Models for Information Technology Security, Gaithersburg, MD, 2001.

[5] T. Bayer and C. Reich, "Security of mobile agents in distributed java agent development framework (JADE) platforms security of mobile agents in distributed java agent development framework (JADE) platforms," no. April, 2017.

[6] S. Bijani and D. Robertson, "A review of attacks and security approaches in open multi-agent systems," *Artif. Intell. Rev.*, vol. 42, no. 4, pp. 607–636, Dec. 2014.

[7] S. Alami-Kamouri, G. Orhanou, and S. Elhajji, "Overview of mobile agents and security," in *Proceedings—The International Conference on Engineering & MIS (ICEMIS)*, 2016.

[8] M. Kaur and S. Saxena, "A review of security techniques for mobile agents," 2017, pp. 807–812.

[9] N. Borselius, "Security in multi-agent systems," no. April, 2014.

[10] B. Amro, "Mobile agent systems, recent security threats and counter measures."

[11] J. Liang, J. Jiang, H. Duan, K. Li, T. Wan, and J. Wu, "When HTTPS meets CDN: A case of authentication in delegated service," in *Proceedings—IEEE Symposium on Security and Privacy*, 2014, pp. 67–82.

[12] K. Bhargavan, C. Fournet, M. Kohlweiss, A. Pironti, and P. Y. Strub, "Implementing TLS with verified cryptographic security," in *Proceedings—IEEE Symposium on Security and Privacy*, 2013, pp. 445–459.

[13] P. Kocher, "Internet Engineering Task Force (IETF) A. Freier request for comments: 6101 P. Karlton Category: Historic Netscape Communications," 2011.

[14] A. Castro-Castilla, "Traffic analysis of an SSL/TLS session - The Blog of Fourthbit," 2014. [Online]. Available: http://blog.fourthbit.com/2014/12/23/traffic-analysis-of-an-ssl-slash-tls-session. [Accessed: 11-Aug-2018].

[15] IETF, "Full-text," *Internet Eng. Task Force*, 2018.

[16] S. Turner, "Transport layer security," *IEEE Internet Comput.*, vol. 18, no. 6, pp. 60–63, Nov. 2014.

[17] X. Vila, A. Schuster, and A. Riera, "Security for a multi-agent system based on JADE," *Comput. Secur.*, vol. 26, no. 5, pp. 391–400, Aug. 2007.

[18] S. Berkovits, J. D. Guttman, and V. Swarup, "Authentication for mobile agents," *Mob. Agents Secur., LNCS*, vol. 1419, pp. 114–136, 1998.

[19] L. Ismail and U. A. Emirates, "Authentication mechanisms for mobile agents Leila Ismail United Arab Emirates University," 2007.

[20] S. Hanaoui, Y. Berguig, and J. Laassiri, On the Security Communication and Migration in Mobile Agent Systems, Springer, Cham, 2019, pp. 302–313.

7 Estimation of Daily Energy Production of a Solar Power Plant Using Artificial Intelligence Techniques

Anass Zaaoumi[1], Hajar Hafs[1], Abdellah Bah[1], Mohammed Alaoui[1], and Abdellah Mechaqrane[2]
[1] Mohammed V University, Rabat, Morocco
[2] Sidi Mohamed Ben Abdellah University, Fez, Morocco

CONTENTS

7.1 INTRODUCTION

Today, energy demand is a growing challenge that humanity faces. Over the centuries, our energy consumption has steadily increased and exploded over the past century. So far, most of our energy is produced from fossil reserves: coal, oil, and gas. Those fossil energies are in one part responsible for the global warming and climatic change, and in other part, these reserves will disappear in the future. It is therefore necessary to use nonfossil energy sources and clean ones.

Long-term alternatives to fossil fuels are renewable energies. Renewable energy resources are clean and inexhaustible. One of the most suitable renewable energies is solar energy. It is clean and free and can perfectly help to solve the problem of climatic change. The most advantageous way to exploit this energy is by concentrating the sunlight in solar plants. A parabolic trough solar thermal power plant (PTSTPP) is one of the concentrated solar power (CSP) technologies that transforms the energy radiated by the sun into heat at high temperature, then into mechanical and electrical energy through a thermodynamic cycle (Cac 2013). Once the energy is captured, the main challenge is to control, manage, and transport it to the electricity grid in compliance with regulations. Unfortunately, solar energy has certain number of intrinsic limitations: production fluctuations or geographical possibilities for implementation. Production fluctuations generate problems on the electricity grid for maintaining the balance between consumption and production. The uncertainty about cloud cover or wind speed and the rapid variation of their production force the manager to compensate by using and increasing the reserves of the energy storage. The storage of energy can stabilize the production of electricity by storing thermal power during periods of high production to restore it when production falls (Guney 2016). However, energy storage reduces efficiency and increases the costs of the power plant. Energy forecasting helps to anticipate the availability of generation sources and thus facilitates the management of the grid. The forecasting methods are based on historical data. Generally, forecasting tools are based on artificial intelligence algorithms like fuzzy logic, neural network, genetic algorithm, or a combination of two techniques.

Many studies applied artificial intelligence methods like artificial neural networks (ANNs) and adaptative neuro-fuzzy inference system (ANFIS) to forecast the energy production. In (Almonacid et al. 2009), the authors use a multilayer perceptron (MLP) neural network with two inputs: temperature and irradiance, to predict the power produced by a photovoltaic (PV) installation. An ANFIS with an echo state network (ESN) for short-term PV power prediction was developed and compared in (Jayawardene et al. 2015). Forecasting the energy production of a PV resource by using artificial intelligence techniques such feed-forward and an Elman neural network was explored in (Dumitru et al. 2016).

Other studies that use ANN and ANFIS models to predict the energy production like solar, wind, and hydraulic systems can be found in (Ihya et al. 2014; Kassa et al. 2016; Dumitru et al. 2017; Hammid et al. 2018).

In this work, we used ANN and ANFIS methods to predict the daily electric production of a solar power plant located at Ain Beni-Mathar (northeast of Morocco) using the structure of the past to predict the future. For input data we used daily time step climatic data in addition to the previous daily time step energy production. Data from 1 November 2011 until 31 December 2015 were used to train and validate the models. The data are presented as a time series, and forecasting time series data is an integral component for management, planning, and decision-making. Comparisons were made between the two techniques in order to define their prediction accuracy.

The paper is organized as follows. Section 7.2.1 presents the description of the solar power plant. Section 7.2.3 devoted to the methods used for the estimation. Section 7.3 presents the study results of the work carried out. Finally, conclusions are presented.

7.2 MATERIALS AND METHODS

7.2.1 DESCRIPTION OF THE SOLAR POWER PLANT

The Ain Beni-Mathar Integrated Solar Combined Cycle Power Plant (ISCC) (Figure 7.1) consists of a PTSTPP and a natural gas-fired combined cycle (NGCC) power plant (Alqahtani et al. 2016). Solar irradiation contributes to increase the total power of the plant up to 20 MW. The study focused on the electric production that comes from the PTSTPP.

At the power plant location, the daily DNI (considered as the sum of DNI on the day) varies from 3.08 KWh/m^2 in November to 8.86 KWh/m^2 in June; the monthly average ambient temperature varies from 5.2°C in February to 30°C in August; the monthly evolution of the average wind speed varies from 1.73 m/s in December to 5.4 m/s in February, while the monthly average relative humidity varies from 21.8% in August to 77% in December (Zaaoumi et al. 2018).

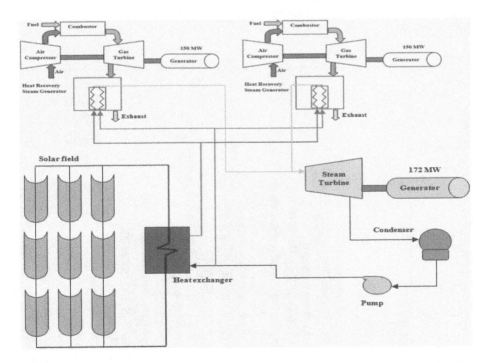

FIGURE 7.1 Components of the integrated solar combined cycle power plant in Ain Beni-Mathar.

7.2.2 ENERGY PRODUCED BY THE PTSTPP

The solar energy harvested by the collectors is concentrated in a metal pipe inside a vacuum glass tube. Inside the pipe, the heat transfer fluid (HTF) is circulated and heated to a temperature of 400°C. This fluid is then pumped through a conventional heat exchanger to produce steam at high temperatures and pressures. The produced steam is used in a Rankine cycle to produce electrical energy through the generator coupled to the steam turbine.

The thermal power at the heat exchanger (Q [W]) is given by the equation:

$$Q_{th} = \dot{m}_{HTF}.C_{p,HTF}.\Delta T \tag{7.1}$$

$\dot{m}_{HTF}$ [kg/s] is the mass flow rate of the HTF, $C_{p,HTF}$ is the heat capacity [J/kg K] of the HTF, ΔT is the HTF temperature difference measured between the inlet and the outlet at the heat exchanger [°C].

The contribution of the solar field in the total electrical energy produced by the plant (E [Wh]) can be determined considering the global efficiency of the heat conversion into electricity $\eta_g = 0.26$:

$$Q_{ele} = \eta_g.Q_{th} \tag{7.2}$$

We try to predict the electrical energy production using ANN and ANFIS models. Figure 7.2 shows the electrical energy production of the power plant over four years (2012–2015).

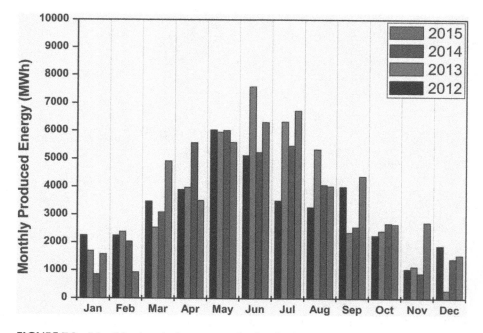

FIGURE 7.2 Monthly electrical energy production for four years.

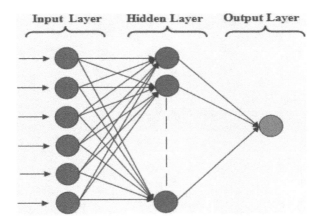

FIGURE 7.3   Structure of ANN model with six input variables.

7.2.3 METHOD

In this study, ANN and ANFIS methods are applied to estimate the daily energy production of a PTSTPP located at Ain Beni-Mathar.

7.2.3.1 Artificial Neural Networks

ANNs are data-processing systems based on the working mechanism of the biological neural system. ANNs are used to solve different problems in science and engineering, particularly in some fields where the conventional modeling methods fail (Najafi et al. 2009).

The MLPs are the most popular type of ANNs. The majority of MLP models developed are three layered, as indicated in Figure 7.3. The first layer corresponds to the import input of the signals. The second layer is defined as the hidden layer that allows receiving and processing of the input variables using the transfer functions. The third layer corresponds to the output layer, which consists of the output units of the network.

Before their use, ANNs must be well trained to anticipate connection parameters. To train a network, the algorithm of back propagation (BP) of the gradient is the most often used method (Boukelia et al. 2017).

7.2.3.2 Adaptative Neuro-Fuzzy Inference System

ANFIS allows the application of ANN and fuzzy logic together (Jang 1993). It belongs to the family of hybrid systems. ANFIS is a combination of two artificial intelligence methods, which uses the benefit of both methods. The structure of ANFIS supports the Takagi–Sugeno-based systems (Takagi et al. 1985). The architecture of the adaptive network has five network layers (Figure 7.4).

Analyzing the mapping relation between the input and output data, ANFIS can establish the optimal distribution of membership functions using either a BP gradient descent algorithm alone or in combination with a least-squares method.

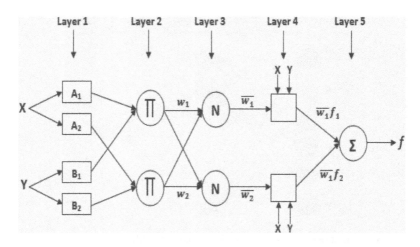

FIGURE 7.4   Adaptive neuro-fuzzy inference system structure.

7.2.3.3   Estimation of Prediction Error

In order to select the best model, the models' performances were evaluated using regular comparison tools in modeling: the coefficient of determination (R), root mean square error (RMSE), and mean absolute error (MAE).

$$R = \frac{\sum_{k=1}(y_k - \bar{y}).(t_k - \bar{t})}{\sqrt{\sum_{k=1}(y_k - \bar{y})^2 . \sum_{k=1}(t_k - \bar{t})^2}} \tag{7.3}$$

$$RMSE = \sqrt{\frac{1}{N} . \sum_{k=1}(t_k - \bar{t})^2} \tag{7.4}$$

$$MAE = \frac{1}{N} . \sum_{k=1}|(t_k - y_k)| \tag{7.5}$$

y_k and t_k denote, respectively, the network output and the measured value for the kth element.

7.2.3.4   Data Normalization

In order to enhance the network prediction processing, all the measured data involving electric energy production, direct normal irradiation, ambient temperature, wind speed, and relative humidity values, collected at Ain Beni-Mathar station, were normalized between 0 and 1 according to the following equation.

$$X_i = \frac{X_{ki} - \min(X_k)}{\max(X_k) - \min(X_k)} \tag{7.6}$$

where X_i is the ith normalized value, and X_{ki} is the ith input of the vector $X_k = (X_{k1}, \ldots, X_{kn})$ that we will normalize.

7.3 RESULTS AND DISCUSSION

The aim of our study is to use and compare ANN and ANFIS models in order to predict the daily electric energy generation of a PTSTPP. The input variables are daily direct normal irradiation (DNI), day of the month (D_m), daily average ambient temperature (t), daily average relative humidity (H_r), daily average wind speed (W_s), and daily previous production (E_{t-1}), while the daily electric energy production is the output variable. To train and validate the models, the MATLAB platform was used.

The dataset used in this study covers a period of more than four years between 1 November 2011 and 31 December 2015. The data were divided in two phases: training and validation; data between 1 November 2011 and 31 December 2014 were used for training phase, and for the validation procedure, we used the data of the year 2015. In this study, we have undergone a detailed processing of the data, and only the data where there is energy production have been considered. It is well noted that there are days where there is no solar energy production because of not enough solar irradiation or the maintenance of solar components. So, we eliminated those data to have a model that links the variation of the input parameters with the variation of energy generation.

For the ANN model, the network was trained and validated by using Levenberg–Marquardt BP algorithm (Table 7.1). We selected this algorithm because it performed the best in the predicting procedure. To choose the best ANN architecture we varied the number of neurons in the hidden layer from 1 to 10.

For the ANFIS model, we used the subtractive clustering as FIS generation method. We varied the numbers of radius between 0.5 and 1 in order to select the best ANFIS architecture that will yield to the best generation result in terms of R, RMSE, and MAE. Table 7.2 shows details about the ANFIS model used in this study.

For both models, we consider that the architecture that gives the best results in terms of R, RMSE, and MAE for validation procedure is the best one. The results obtained from the measurement and the results generated from ANN and ANFIS models are discussed in this article. Table 7.3 shows for each tested ANN architecture, the average performances in terms of R, RMSE, and MAE is 10 runs. The results are promising, and it was found that the architecture that yielded to the best generalization results is the architecture with four hidden neurons. Table 7.4 shows

TABLE 7.1
Parameters of the ANN Model

ANN Info	Parameters
Number of epochs	1000
Training algorithm of network	Back propagation
Type of activation functions	Logsig, tansig

TABLE 7.2
Parameters of the ANFIS Model

ANFIS Info	Characteristics
Fuzzy structure	Sugeno type
Initial FIS for training	Genfis2
Epoch	50
Output membership function	Linear
Training algorithm	Hybrid

TABLE 7.3
Average Performances Obtained for Different Numbers of Hidden Neurons

Hidden Neurons' Number	Training Phase			Validation Phase		
	R	RMSE	MAE	R	RMSE	MAE
1	0.9224	0.0868	0.0634	0.9203	0.0972	0.0716
2	0.9330	0.0809	0.0600	0.9304	0.0943	0.0697
3	0.9396	0.0769	0.0570	0.9386	0.0925	0.0701
4	**0.9451**	**0.0735**	**0.0539**	**0.9408**	**0.0899**	**0.0662**
5	0.9465	0.0725	0.0531	0.9362	0.0906	0.0684
6	0.9494	0.0706	0.0509	0.9389	0.0896	0.0654
7	0.9503	0.0699	0.0508	0.9369	0.0907	0.0661
8	0.9516	0.0691	0.0501	0.9335	0.0912	0.0658
9	0.9536	0.0676	0.0490	0.9380	0.0901	0.0660
10	0.9554	0.0663	0.0484	0.9330	0.0925	0.0685

TABLE 7.4
Average Performances Obtained for Different Numbers of Radius

Number of Radius	Training Phase			Validation Phase		
	R	RMSE	MAE	R	RMSE	MAE
0,50	0.9672	0.0571	0.0415	0.9099	0.1028	0.0759
0,55	0.9650	0.0590	0.0431	0.9139	0.0975	0.0717
0,60	0.9619	0.0615	0.0443	0.9218	0.0974	0.0721
0,65	0.9553	0.0664	0.0480	0.9213	0.0984	0.0741
0,70	0.9534	0.0678	0.0484	0.9355	0.0912	0.0686
0,75	0.9531	0.0680	0.0488	0.9361	0.0916	0.0685
0,80	0.9519	0.0688	0.0497	0.9299	0.0963	0.0703
0,85	0.9483	0.0713	0.0513	0.9375	0.0895	0.0668
0,90	**0.9481**	**0.0714**	**0.0514**	**0.9377**	**0.0893**	**0.0664**
0,95	0.9427	0.0749	0.0551	0.9373	0.0903	0.0670
1.00	0.9426	0.0750	0.0553	0.9368	0.0907	0.0677

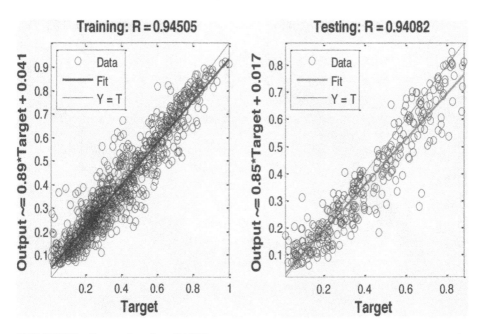

FIGURE 7.5 Regression plot of ANN.

for each tested ANFIS architecture the average performances in terms of R, RMSE, and MAE for different numbers of radius. It is noticed that the best architecture was obtained with radius = 0.9.

Figure 7.5 shows the regression plots, respectively, for the ANN model. For training phase, the value of regression is R = 0.945, and for the validation phase, R = 0.948. Figure 7.6 presents the regression plot for the ANFIS model. The values of regression are R = 0.94 and R = 0.937, respectively, for the training and validation phases.

In this part, we will compare the results obtained from PTSTPP electric energy production using ANN and ANFIS models. Figures 7.7 and 7.8 show a comparison of the energy production between the measured ANN and ANFIS models, respectively, for the training and validation phases. It is observed from both figures that the different energy production curves follow the same trends with a minor difference, which means that both ANN and ANFIS models can predict the energy production.

In order to have a good observation of the energy production curves, we applied a zoom on Figures 7.7 and 7.8. A continuous 10 days were considered from different years of the study. For the training phase, the years are 2012 (Figure 7.9-a), 2013 (Figure 7.9-b), and 2014 (Figure 7.9-c). The year 2015 (Figure 7.9-d) was considered for the validation phase; we associated together the absolute values of prediction errors for training and validation days. It is well noticed that both ANN and ANFIS models provide curves that perfectly follow the shape of real ones, despite amplitude default in some points, thus, demonstrate the capability of the proposed models to predict the electric energy production of PTSTPP.

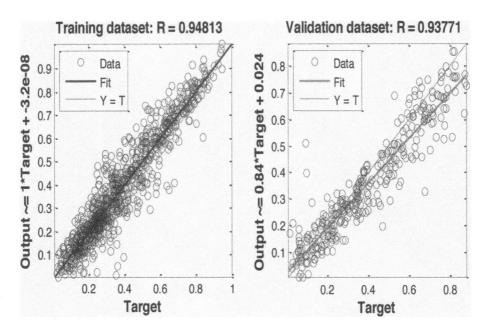

FIGURE 7.6 Regression plot of ANFIS.

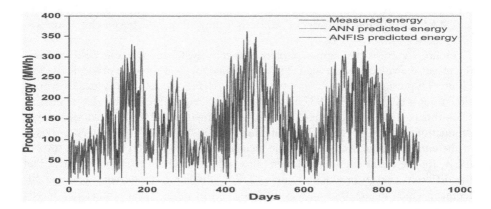

FIGURE 7.7 Comparison between measured, ANN, and ANFIS predicted energy production—training set.

A comparison between monthly ANN, ANFIS predicted, and measured electric energy production for the solar plant is presented in Figure 7.10. The total yearly ANN and ANFIS predicted energy productions are, respectively, 39,341 MWh/year and 39,907 MWh/year for the validation year (2015). The real production is about 44,138 MWh/year. The predicted energy production underestimates with approximately 10.86% for the ANN model and about 9.58% for the ANFIS model.

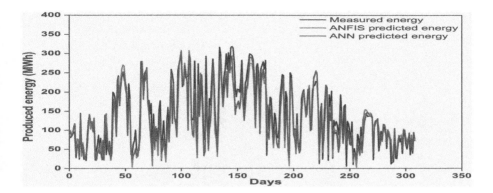

FIGURE 7.8 Comparison between measured, ANN, and ANFIS predicted energy production—validation set.

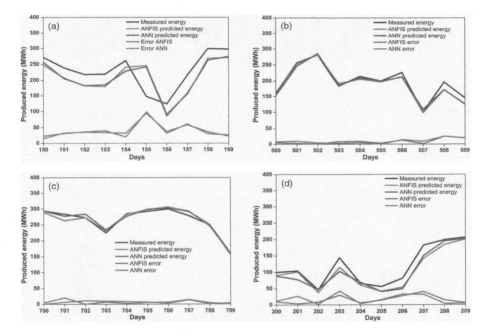

FIGURE 7.9 (a) Zoom on measured and predicted energy—training set (2012). (b) Zoom on measured and predicted energy—training set (2013). (c) Zoom on measured and predicted energy—training set (2014). (d) Zoom on measured and predicted energy—validation set (2015).

The monthly errors between ANN, ANFIS predicted, and measured values of the electric energy produced by the solar power plant are presented in Figure 7.11. For the ANN model, the highest absolute error value of about 21.3% was noticed in October and the lowest value of about 1.2% was noticed in November. For the ANFIS model, the highest absolute error value of about 22% was noticed in April and the lowest value of about 1.7% was noticed in February.

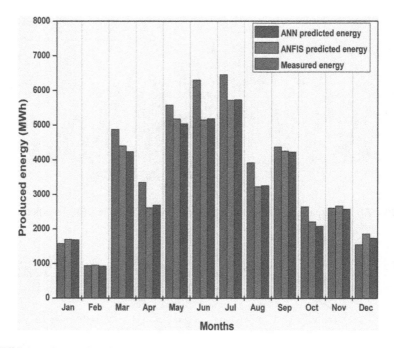

FIGURE 7.10   Comparison between ANN, ANFIS predicted, and measured energy production.

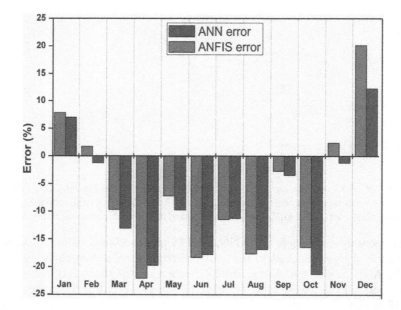

FIGURE 7.11   Monthly error for the validation year.

7.4 CONCLUSION

In this paper, we have estimated the daily electric energy production of a PTSTPP using ANN and ANFIS methods. The ANN and ANFIS models were developed considering six input variables (daily DNI, daily average ambient temperature, time in function of day of the month, daily average relative humidity, daily average wind speed, and daily previous energy production) and one output data. The estimated values for the ANN and ANFIS models were found to be close to the real ones with values of regression about $R = 0.94$ for the validation phase. ANFIS underestimated the yearly energy production by 9.58% with monthly absolute errors in the range of 1.7% to 22%. ANN underestimated the yearly energy production by 10.86% with monthly absolute errors in the range of 1.2 to 21.3%. Based on the obtained results, it can be concluded that ANN and ANFIS models can successfully estimate the PTSTPP energy production.

ACKNOWLEDGMENTS

The authors wish to express their sincere thanks to Mr. Mohammed Berrehili from Office National de l'Electricité et de l'Eau Potable (ONEE) for sharing the data, without which this work would not have been possible.

REFERENCES

Almonacid, F., C. Rus, P. J. Pérez, and L. Hontoria. 2009. Estimation of the energy of a PV generator using artificial neural network. *Renewable Energy* 34(12):2743–50.

Alqahtani, B. J., and D. Patiño-Echeverri. 2016. Integrated solar combined cycle power plants: Paving the way for thermal solar. *Applied Energy* 169:927–36.

Boukelia, T. E., O. Arslan, and M. S. Mecibah. 2017. Potential assessment of a parabolic trough solar thermal power plant considering hourly analysis: ANN-based approach. *Renewable Energy* 105:324–33.

Cac, G. 2013. Concentrated solar power plants: Review and design methodology. *Renewable and Sustainable Energy Reviews* 22:466–81.

Dumitru, C. D., A. Gligor, and C. Enachescu. 2016. Solar photovoltaic energy production forecast using neural networks. *Procedia Technology* 22:808–15.

Dumitru, C. D., and A. Gligor. 2017. Daily average wind energy forecasting using artificial neural networks. *Procedia Engineering* 181:829–36.

Guney, M. S. 2016. Solar power and application methods. *Renewable and Sustainable Energy Reviews* 57:776–85.

Hammid, A. T., M. H. Bin Sulaiman, and A. N. Abdalla. 2018. Prediction of small hydropower plant power production in Himreen Lake dam (HLD) using artificial neural network. *Alexandria Engineering Journal* 57:211–21.

Ihya, B., A. Mechaqrane, R. Tadili, and M. N. Bargach. 2014. Prediction of hourly and daily diffuse solar fraction in the city of Fez (Morocco). *Theoretical and Applied Climatology* 120(3–4):737–49.

Jang, J. R. 1993. ANFIS: Adaptive-network-based fuzzy inference system. *IEEE Transactions on Systems, Man and Cybernetics* 23(3):665–85.

Jayawardene, I., and G. K. Venayagamoorthy. 2015. Comparison of adaptive neuro-fuzzy inference systems and echo state networks for PV power prediction. *Procedia Computer Science* 53(1):92–102.

Kassa, Y., J. Zhang, D. Zheng, and D. Wei. 2016. Short term wind power prediction using ANFIS. *IEEE International Conference on Power and Renewable Energy (ICPRE)* 388–93.

Najafi, G., B. Ghobadian, T. Tavakoli, D. R. Buttsworth, T. F. Yusaf, and M. Faizollahnejad. 2009. Performance and exhaust emissions of a gasoline engine with ethanol blended gasoline fuels using artificial neural network. *Applied Energy* 86(5):630–39.

Takagi, T, and M. Sugeno. 1985. Fuzzy identification of systems and its applications to modeling and control. *IEEE Transactions on Systems, Man and Cybernetics* 15(1):116–32.

Zaaoumi, A., A. Bah, M. Alaoui, A. Mechaqrane, and M. Berreheli. 2018. Application of artificial neural networks and adaptive neuro-fuzzy inference system to estimate the energy generation of a solar power plant in Ain Beni-Mathar (Morocco). *10th International Conference on Electronics, Computers and Artificial Intelligence* 1–6.

8 Daily Time Series Estimation of Global Horizontal Solar Radiation from Artificial Neural Networks

Mebrouk Bellaoui, Kada Bouchouicha,
Nouar Aoun, Ibrahim Oulimar,
and Abdeldjabar Babahadj
Unité de Recherche en Energies Renouvelables
en Milieu Saharien, UERMS
Centre de Développement des Energies
Renouvelables, Adrar, Algeria

CONTENTS

8.1 INTRODUCTION

Energy assessment requires measurements and comprehensive data collection in the best conditions. Several studies have been conducted on the evaluation of solar radiation by models in order to generate artificial sequences of radiometric data.

Artificial intelligence (AI) is a term that explains, in its broadest sense, the ability of a machine to perform functions similar to those that characterize human thought.

AI techniques are grouped into five branches: neural networks, fuzzy logic, genetic algorithms, expert system, and hybrid system (Mohandes, 1998; Mubiru and Banda, 2008).

The aim of our work is to use neural models to estimate the global daily radiation at the renewable energy research unit station in the Saharan environment in order to obtain a reliable database.

8.2 MODEL DESCRIPTION

8.2.1 Artificial Neural Network

The artificial neural network (ANN) is a system inspired by theories and observation of the neural structure and functioning of the human nervous system. ANN is a programed computational nonlinear model that is widely used in the field of solar energy for design, modeling, and optimization of solar projects.

ANN is a part of AI, which represents a computational model that has the capability to learn from observational data. The ANN model usually can be divided into three parts, called layers: the input layer, which is responsible for receiving the input data which must be normalized before being used; the second layer is hidden layer that contains a nonlinear transfer function; and the third layer produces the output (Mellit et al, 2005; Mellit, 2008).

In teaching an ANN that is being reduced to an optimization problem (Figure 8.1), we find the minimum of an error function, so that we can build on this method of universal optimization gradient descent, which will be the gradient backpropagation rule for multilayer networks, studied in the following sections (Azadeh et al, 2009).

8.2.2 Learning Algorithm

Let p and t be the target input and output vectors used for network learning and a be the network response. The objective is to minimize the cost function F (mean squared error between inputs and network responses) (Rahimikhoob, 2010; Cyril, 2011) defined as:

$$F = \frac{1}{Q}\sum_{k=1}^{Q}\left[t(k) - a(k)\right]^2 = \frac{1}{Q}\sum_{k=1}^{Q}\left[e(k)\right]^2 \qquad (8.1)$$

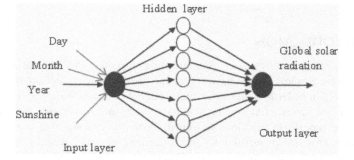

FIGURE 8.1   Neuronal network model.

Q is the number of examples. This minimization is done according to a delta rule:

$$\Delta w = -\infty \frac{\partial f}{\partial w} \tag{8.2}$$

The least mean square (LMS) algorithm estimates the kth iteration of the mean squared error e^2 by calculating the derivative of the mean squared errors in relation to the network weight and bias. So:

$$\begin{cases} \dfrac{\partial e^2(k)}{\partial w_j} = 2e(k)\dfrac{\partial e(k)}{\partial w_j} \quad j = 1...R \\[4mm] \dfrac{\partial e^2(k)}{\partial b} = 2e(k)\dfrac{\partial e(k)}{\partial b} \end{cases} \tag{8.3}$$

Or

$$\frac{\partial e(k)}{\partial w_j} = \frac{\partial[t(k) - a(k)]}{\partial w_j} = \frac{\partial[t(k) - w_p(k) + b]}{\partial w_j} = \frac{\partial t(k)}{\partial w_j} - \frac{\partial\left[\sum_{i=1}^{R} w_i p_i(k) + b\right]}{\partial w_j}$$

Simplified:

$$\begin{cases} \dfrac{\partial e(k)}{\partial w_j} = -p_j(k) \quad j = 1...R \\[4mm] \dfrac{\partial e(k)}{b} = -1 \end{cases} \tag{8.4}$$

This means that the weights and biases of the network must change:

$$2 \propto e(k)p(k) \; et \; 2 \propto e(k) \tag{8.5}$$

where α is the learning rate. For the case of several neurons, we can write the equation as:

$$\begin{cases} w(k+1) = w(k) + 2 \propto e(k)p^T(k) \\ b(k+1) = b(k) + 2 \propto e(k) \end{cases} \tag{8.6}$$

Multilayer perceptron (MLP), or layered networks, form the vast majority of networks. They are timeless (static and not dynamic networks).

8.3 DATABASE PRESENTATION

The data we used in our application are global insolation measurements of the Adrar site (latitude 27.87, longitude −0.272).

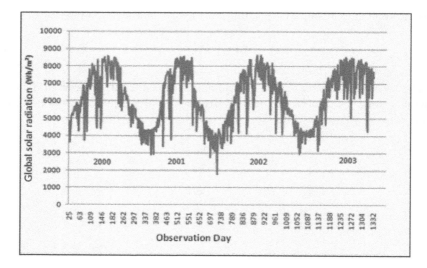

FIGURE 8.2   Daily data of global solar irradiation horizontal 2000–2003, Adrar area.

The geographical coordinates of Adrar are as follows:

- Altitude: 278 m.
- Latitude: 27° 52 North.
- Longitude: 00° 17 West.

The database has been divided into two subsets; the first is used to perform the learning and the other set to do the test. The first contains four years from 2000 to 2003 (Figure 8.2), and the second a two-year set from June 2003 to June 2005 to test (Figure 8.3).

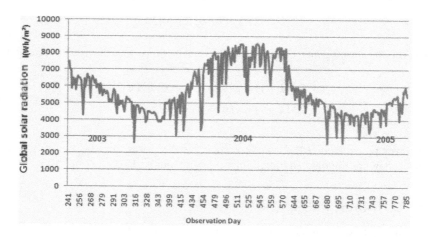

FIGURE 8.3   Daily data of global solar irradiation horizontal 2003–2005, Adrar area.

8.4 THE MODEL USED

The model used to estimate global solar radiation on a horizontal plane is the modified form of the Angstrom equation. This regression equation relates the average fraction of daily radiation by the radiation in a clear sky and the average fraction of duration of sunshine (Angstrom, 1924; Prescott, 1940; Page, 1961; Duffie and Beckman, 1991).

$$\frac{H}{H_0} = a + b\frac{S}{S_0} \tag{8.7}$$

H: daily global solar radiation.
H_0: extraterrestrial solar radiation.
S: sunshine durations.
S_0: astronomical duration of the day.
a and b are empirical coefficients.

$$H_0 = \frac{24}{\pi} I_{sc} \left[1 + 0.033 \cos\frac{360n}{365} \right]$$

$$\left[\cos\phi\cos\delta\sin\omega_s + \frac{\pi}{180}\omega_s\sin\phi\sin\delta \right] \tag{8.8}$$

Isc: the solar constant (= 1367 Wm2).
φ: latitude of site, δ: solar declination.
ω: sunrise angle.

$$\delta = 23.45\sin\frac{360(284+n)}{365} \tag{8.9}$$

$$\omega_s = \cos^{-1}\left(-\tan\phi\tan\delta\right) \tag{8.10}$$

The maximum sunshine duration S_0 can be calculated as follows:

$$s_0 = \frac{12}{15}\omega_s \tag{8.11}$$

8.5 SIMUATION RESULTS

For learning purposes, we used the measured data during the period 2000–2003 (Figure 8.4).

The correlation coefficient for the forecast R = 0.81651.

The correlation coefficient for the forecast R = 0.76259.

The mean squared error graph (Figure 8.5) shows that the Levenberg–Marquardt algorithm gives satisfactory results, and the error is less than 0.7.

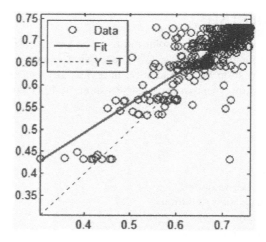

FIGURE 8.4 Learning phase (first step).

The correlation coefficient for the forecast R = 0.73512.

The function represents an approximation of the correlation between predicted and desired outputs (see Figures 8.6, 8.7 and 8.8); according to the data used, the coefficient is approximately 0.78, so we can improve on the model to get better results.

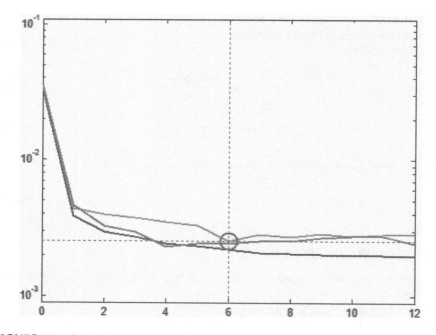

FIGURE 8.5 Quadratic mean error. Curves in red (a), green (b), and blue (c) represent learning, validation, and test, respectively.

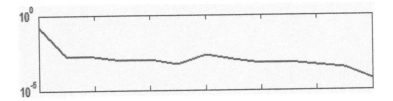

FIGURE 8.6   Gradient = 4.8735e-005 for 12 iterations.

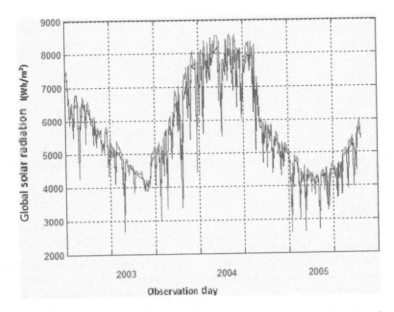

FIGURE 8.7   Global horizontal solar radiation estimated from a sunshine duration of the 2003–2005 period, in red (a) the desired outputs, in blue (b) the predicted outputs (simulated).

8.6   CONCLUSIONS

In our study, we were interested in the neural network prediction method, in particular, the MLP method.

For learning purposes, we used the Levenberg–Marquardt algorithm to calculate the weight approximation. For this network, the inputs propagate to the output without return.

For the learning, we used the database from 2000–2003; for the test, we used the data from 2003–2005; the simulation with these databases gives results of correlation coefficient equal to 0.81651 for learning and 0.76259 for validation. According to the correlation graphs between the desired and predicted outputs, on the one hand, and the mean squared error, on the other, we can use this neural model to estimate daily global solar irradiations.

Improving the model with the use of the data from the Adrar URERMS research unit station remains a work for the future.

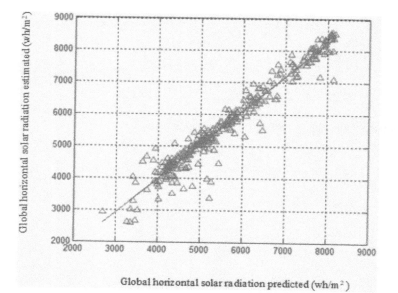

FIGURE 8.8   The correlation between the desired outputs and predicted outputs of global horizontal solar radiation.

REFERENCES

Angstrom, A., 1924. Solar and terrestrial radiation, *The Quarterly Journal of the Royal Meteorological Society* 50:121–5.

Azadeh, A., Maghsoudi, A., Sohrabkhani, S., 2009. An integrated artificial neural networks approach for predicting global radiation, *Energy Conversion Management* 50(6):1497–505.

Cyril, V., 2011. Prédiction de séries temporelles de rayonnement solaireglobal et de production d'énergie photovoltaïque à partirde réseaux de neurones artificiels, *Université de corse-pascal paoli. Thèse doctorat.*

Duffie, J. A., Beckman, W. A., 1991. Solar engineering of thermal process. New York: Wiley.

Mellit, A., 2008. Artificial Intelligence technique for modelling and forecasting of solar radiation data, *International Journal of Artificial Intelligence and Soft Computing* 1(1):69–75.

Mellit, A., Benghanem, M., Hadj Arab, A., Guessoum, A., 2005. A simplified model for generating sequences of global solar radiation data for isolated sites: Using artificial neural network and a library of Markov transition matrices approach, *Solar Energy* 79:469–82.

Mohandes, M., Rehman, S., Halawani, T. O., 1998. Estimation of global solar radiation using artificial neural networks, *Renewable Energy* 14:179–84.

Mubiru, J., Banda, E. J. K. B., 2008. Estimation of monthly average daily global solar irradiation using artificial neural networks, *Solar Energy* 82:181–7.

Page, J. K., 1961. The estimation of monthly mean values of daily total short wave radiation on vertical and inclined surfaces from sunshine records for latitudes 40N–40S. In: *Proceedings of UN conference on new sources of energy* 78–90.

Prescott, J. A., 1940. Evaporation from water surface in relation to solar radiation. *Transactions of the Royal Society of Australia* 46:114–8.

Rahimikhoob, A., 2010. Estimating global solar radiation using artificial neural network and air temperature data in a semi-arid environment, *Renewable Energy* 35:2131–5.

9 Credit Default Swaps between Past, Present, and Future

Nadir Oumayma and Daoui Driss
Ibn Tofail University, Kenitra, Morocco

CONTENTS

9.1 INTRODUCTION

Credit default swaps (CDS) were engineered in 1994 by the US bank J. P. Morgan, Inc., to transfer credit risk exposure from its balance sheet to protection sellers. At that time, hardly anyone could have imagined the extent to which CDS would occupy the daily lives of traders, regulators, and financial economists alike in the twenty-first century. As of this writing, more than 1,000 working papers posted on the Social Science Research Network are directly related to the economic role of CDS or involve CDS as a research tool in one way or another. Nevertheless, some key issues on CDS are still hotly debated. In a recent monograph (Augustin et al. 2014), we surveyed the extant literature, which keeps growing even as we write.

In that broad survey, we covered a variety of research domains, ranging from cross-asset pricing effects, to corporate finance applications, to the role of CDS in financial intermediation, among many other topics. In this review, our goal is to elaborate on our views about future research directions in the context of the received literature, rather than to comprehensively survey the existing work. In so doing, we will focus on the issues that need more dedicated attention and that represent fruitful areas for investigation in the years to come.

We first discuss the welfare implications of CDS for corporations, financial intermediaries, and regulators. We then discuss some recent rules and market developments. Because many such issues are in the confluence of law and finance, we explain some of the technical aspects as well. Given recent events in Greece, Argentina, and Puerto Rico, we place considerable emphasis on analyzing the role of CDS in the context of sovereign risk and international finance. Currently, there are many unwarranted assertions on the perverse effects of CDS with little recognition of their salutary consequences. We hope to correct some misperceptions and to present a more balanced view of the relevant issues about CDS.

9.2   THE WELFARE IMPLICATIONS OF CDS TRADING

CDS contracts have been widely castigated as being among the main causes of the US subprime crisis in 2007–2008 (which led to the global meltdown in September 2008) and of the Eurozone sovereign debt crisis in 2010–2011. In the former case, many blamed CDS because their leveraged and flexible nature facilitated the creation of synthetic securitized products such as collateralized debt obligations (CDOs) in, for example, the mortgage-backed securities market in the United States. (For a detailed explanation of the role of CDS during the financial crisis, see Stulz 2010; for a discussion of how CDS helped burst the housing bubble, see Fostel & Geanakoplos 2015.) In the latter case, some commentators have discredited CDS as vehicles for speculating against other investors' or governments' assets by accelerating default on the underlying debt.

Other studies seek to understand whether the existence of CDS affects firm characteristics or whether it changes the behavioral incentives of firms or financial intermediaries. However, these studies typically focus on only one particular aspect of the economy and usually examine the cost–benefit analysis from a partial equilibrium perspective. Next, we review part of the literature along the following three dimensions: impacts of CDS on asset prices, liquidity, and efficiency; on firm characteristics and economic incentives; and on financial intermediaries and the debtor–creditor relationship.

Figure 9.1 represents the CDS by type of position in billions of US dollars.

9.3   IMPACT OF CDS ON ASSET PRICES,
LIQUIDITY, AND EFFICIENCY

The existing research has examined the effect of CDS on both parts of the capital structure, that is, bonds and equity. Concerning bonds, Nashikkar, Subrahmanyam & Mahanti (2011), for example, document liquidity spillovers from CDS to the pricing

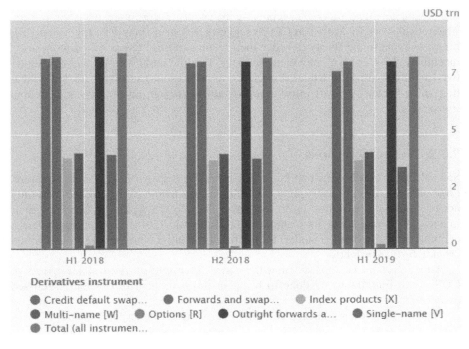

FIGURE 9.1   Notional amounts outstanding overview.

and liquidity in the corresponding bond market. In terms of pricing effects, Das, Kalimipalli & Nayak (2014) and Massa & Zhang (2012) provide opposing views. Whereas the former case finds that CDS trading hurts bond market efficiency, quality, and liquidity because the alternative trading venue substitutes for bond trading, the latter argues that the existence of CDS improves bond liquidity, as the ability to hedge reduces the fire sale risk when bonds get downgraded to junk status. Ashcraft & Santos (2009) suggest that the initiation of CDS trading can have a screening benefit, as the effect of CDS initiation depends on the borrower's credit quality; it reduces borrowing costs for creditworthy borrowers and increases them for risky and informationally opaque firms. Kim (2013), however, argues that it is those firms with high strategic default incentives that benefit from a relatively larger reduction in their corporate bond spreads, and the evidence in Asia provided by Shim & Zhu (2014) points toward a more modest discount in yield spreads at issuance due to CDS trading initiation.

9.3.1   IMPACT OF CDS ON FIRM CHARACTERISTICS
AND ECONOMIC INCENTIVES

Another strand of research has examined the impact of CDS trading from a corporate finance perspective. In particular, this literature examines how the existence of CDS affects default risk and bankruptcy costs, as well as how this change in firm characteristics alters the economic behavior of corporate decision-makers. Theoretical work by Morrison (2005) suggests that firms may face higher borrowing costs because the ability to hedge their credit exposure reduces their monitoring incentives. This, in turn, may increase firms' funding costs with respect to alternative funding sources, in which companies do not benefit from the bank's certification value because of soft information obtained through an arm's-length lending transaction.

9.3.2 FUTURE DIRECTIONS

Several broad conclusions can be drawn from this survey of the extant literature. First, although it is generally recognized that the economic environment is certainly not frictionless, it is important to recognize the role of specific frictions and their impact on interest costs, by Oehmke & Zawadowski (2016) on who implement a calibration of a dynamic model. Fully structural estimations in the future would provide further insights.

Although there is some existing theoretical literature on the welfare effects of CDS, more remains to be done to bring in the additional dimensions discussed earlier.

Figure 9.2 represents stacked column of derivatives counterparty country.

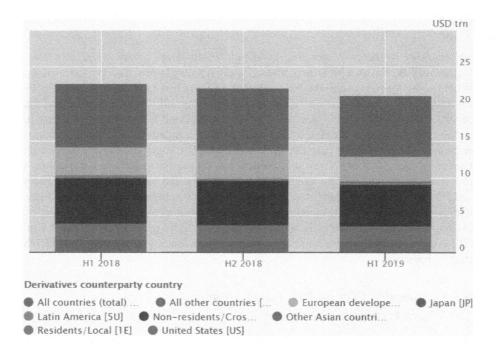

FIGURE 9.2   Credit default swaps by location of counterparty.

9.3.3 POSTCRISIS CDS MARKET, DODD–FRANK, AND BASEL III

The most controversial provision of the Dodd–Frank Act with respect to CDS was the swap "push out" rule (Section 716 of the act). According to this rule, commercial banks and bank holding companies would have been required to trade uncleared single-name CDS through a separate subsidiary with higher capital requirements. Notably, however, the "push out" of riskier derivatives such as CDS from deposit-taking institutions was repealed in December 2014.

During the November 2010 Seoul Summit, leaders of the G-20 countries endorsed the new bank capital and liquidity regulations (Basel III) proposed by the Basel Committee on Banking Supervision.

Basel III aimed to close some loopholes that banks have exploited using CDS contracts. The incentives of banks to use CDS to manage regulatory capital are examined by Shan, Tang & Yan (2014) and Yorulmazer (2013). Whereas banks may appear safer (as measured by regulators or bank examiners) if many of their activities are moved off their balance sheets, their portfolio risk could in fact be higher. The aforementioned London Whale case was allegedly caused in part by a reaction to the so-called Basel 2.5 bank capital regulation, which requires banks to have more capital for CDS trading (Watt 2012). Moreover, banks' use of CDS can create systematic risk because banks are both major buyers and sellers of CDS and are usually at the core of the CDS dealer network. Siriwardane (2015) shows that the network has become even more concentrated since the 2007–2008 global financial crisis.

9.4 CDS AND INTERNATIONAL FINANCE

CDS feature several advantages over bonds that make them particularly appealing for financial market research in international settings. They are constant-maturity-spread products with homogeneously defined contracts that are less plagued by issuer-related differences in covenants or legal systems and by country-related differences in legal origins. Thus, they allow for a much cleaner comparison in empirical work across countries and companies than bond yield spreads do.

Further, many of them are denominated in US dollars, mostly removing the currency risk dimension from the analysis. Although some papers make use of international CDS data, papers usually focus on pure pricing implications and are mostly confined to the sovereign context. The use of CDS in international settings as an economic tool for answering corporate finance or asset pricing related questions is, in our opinion, not very developed.[1] One contrasting example is the work by Ang & Longstaff (2013), who, motivated by economic arguments, compare the decomposition of CDS spreads of sovereign states in the United States and sovereign governments in the European Union to draw inferences on the determinants of systemic sovereign credit risk.

Figure 9.3 represents an area of the derivatives' underlying risk sector.

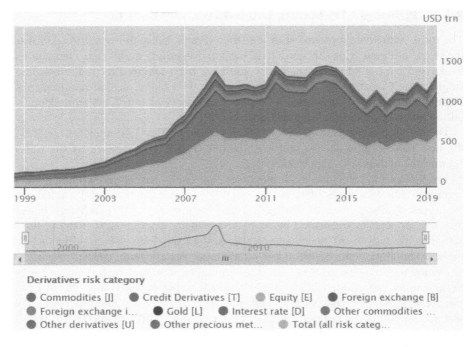

USD trn

1500

1000

500

0

1999   2003   2007   2011   2015   2019

Derivatives risk category

● Commodities [J]   ● Credit Derivatives [T]   ● Equity [E]   ● Foreign exchange [B]
● Foreign exchange i...   ● Gold [L]   ● Interest rate [D]   ● Other commodities ...
● Other derivatives [U]   ● Other precious met...   ● Total (all risk categ...

FIGURE 9.3   Derivatives' risk category.

9.4.1 DETERMINANTS OF SOVEREIGN CREDIT RISK

Ever since the seminal works of Eaton & Gersovitz (1981) and Bulow & Rogoff (1989), academics have tried to understand why governments are able to borrow, despite repeated evidence of sovereign default. With the development of the CDS market, researchers have obtained useful tools with which to also study the cross-country pricing of sovereign credit risk. This is of particular relevance in light of an aging population, a growing pension fund industry, and both banking and insurance regulations that encourage investment in government debt for a range of financial institutions. Thus, understanding the nature of sovereign credit risk and how government debt fits into the investment opportunity set is undeniably important.

To date, the key debate in the literature on sovereign credit risk has circled around the question of whether sovereign credit spreads are determined by global or country-specific risk factors. (For an exhaustive survey, see Augustin et al. 2014.) For most of the time prior to the financial crisis, the empirical evidence suggested that global risk factors were the primary determinants of sovereign credit risk. These risk factors are mostly associated with the United States and are deemed to be either financial (Pan & Singleton 2008; Longstaff et al. 2011) or macroeconomic (Chernov, Schmid & Schneider 2015; Augustin & T'edongap 2016) in nature. Longstaff et al. (2011) even argue that both risk premia and default probabilities are better explained by US financial risk factors than by country-specific fundamentals. The dominant role of global risk factors was essentially justified by the particularly strong comovement of sovereign spreads, at least until the financial crisis.[2]

9.4.2 CORPORATE AND SOVEREIGN CREDIT RISK

International CDS data have also been used to study spillover effects from sovereign onto corporate credit risk. A government's distress may be felt by its nonfinancial corporations, as any financial pain at the level of the sovereign may be passed on through a hike in corporate tax rates, reduced investments in public infrastructure, or lower subsidies, which could harm long-term growth.

Augustin et al. (2015a) exploit the first Greek bailout on April 11, 2010, which was a shock to the sovereign credit risk of all European countries, to document a sovereign-to-corporate risk transfer. Public ownership, financial dependence, and the sovereign ceiling are channels that appear to increase the interdependence between sovereign and corporate credit risk. Bai & Wei (2012) investigate the risk transfer from the sovereign to the corporate sector using a sample of international CDS data from 30 countries.

9.4.3 FUTURE DIRECTIONS

The use of international CDS data is in its infancy, which allows for the future growth of the literature in multiple directions. For now, studies of international CDS have primarily focused on the sovereign context. Although most focus on the level of spreads, using the information embedded in the term structure may prove useful for advancing our understanding of sovereign credit risk from an asset pricing perspective. Getting a precise picture of sovereign risk and rewards will certainly be challenging, but it will be of the utmost importance, given that new regulations such as the naked sovereign CDS ban in Europe have been implemented to prevent negative externalities arising from trading in sovereign CDS contracts. Having said that, we stress that almost all studies on sovereign CDS to date focus exclusively on prices, whereas studying quantities based on trading volumes will be necessary to sharpen our current understanding. Another related agenda, which we feel is currently underresearched, is that of quanto CDS, which places itself at the intersection of two literatures, that of international finance/sovereign risk and that of currency risk premia.

Finally, the use of CDS data as a research tool in international corporate finance is likely the most unexplored area. Thus, combining high-frequency CDS data with equity data in international settings around corporate events such as, for example, mergers and acquisitions, earnings announcements, or cross-listings will help us to answer open questions with respect to capital structure effects and international integration. Along these dimensions, Augustin et al. (2015b) exploit international cross-listings as an exogenous source of variation in capital structure dynamics to show how an increase in information can improve capital structure integration.

9.5   CONCLUSION

There is significant uncertainty about the CDS market, with a major player, Deutsche Bank, having decided to leave the market, and with some observers even claiming that "the CDS market is dead". However, others in the industry think the market is here to stay. For example, Bob Pickel, former chief executive of ISDA, believes that the departure of big investment banks from the CDS market may simply open up opportunities for other players. Indeed, the best-performing hedge fund of 2014, Napier Park Global Capital, made its money by buying CDS, even as banks were reducing their positions. Even though the single-name CDS market has retreated somewhat since the financial crisis, partially because of trade compressions and netting of positions, the market was still worth an impressive $20 trillion at the end of 2014. In our view, the market has proven resilient, despite the reputational losses suffered because of the global credit and sovereign debt crises.

The continuous standardization and regulatory push toward central clearing will likely accelerate the activity in the years to come. CDS can certainly be misused, but they also provide valuable risk-sharing services. Throwing out the baby with the bathwater before having drawn a complete picture of the costs and benefits of trading CDS may be ill-advised.

In this review, we have laid out several research areas that we believe need further and better understanding and that consequently offer fruitful research avenues for the future. Numerous researchers have contributed tremendously to the exponential growth in this literature over the past years. We hope that this momentum continues. CDS are interesting and exciting products, and they have implications that touch upon several policy questions. We hope that academics will continue to push the boundaries of knowledge in this field in the years to come.

9.6   SUMMARY POINTS

1. Although research on CDS has grown tremendously, there remain gaps that offer fruitful directions for future research.
2. CDS contracts have real effects on agency conflicts of financial intermediaries and other economic agents. CDS also have externalities for the prices, liquidity, and efficiency of related markets, including bond, equity, and loan covenants. More research on the overall welfare implications of CDS is needed.
3. The postcrisis CDS market is undergoing structural changes, with a substantial regulatory overhaul, which itself may have a direct impact on the CDS market. The most relevant regulatory changes for CDS include the Volcker Rule, the central clearing of CDS indices, the swap push-out rule under the Dodd–Frank Act, and the new bank capital and liquidity regulations under Basel III.

NOTES

1. One likely reason for the gap in CDS research within the international finance dimension is the lack of CDS databases that are easily mapped into international corporate balance sheet and stock price data. We have encountered this problem ourselves, as we are currently engaged in research on the effects of quantitative easing on corporate decisions, and CDS contracts are clearly a variable of interest in that research.
2. An interesting contribution is also provided by Benzoni et al. (2015), who explain how the comovement in sovereign spreads can arise through contagion. Focusing on US CDS spreads, Chernov, Schmid & Schneider (2015) develop an equilibrium macrofinance model with endogenous default to show that the empirically observed prices for US default insurance are consistent with high risk-adjusted fiscal default probabilities.

REFERENCES

Acharya V. V., Drechsler I., Schnabl P. 2014. A Pyrrhic victory? Bank bailouts and sovereign credit risk. The Journal of Finance 69:2689–2739.

Acharya V. V., Shachar O., Subrahmanyam M. G. 2011. Regulating Wall Street: The Dodd-Frank Act and the new architecture of global finance (Chapter 13), edited by V. V. Acharya, T. Cooley, M. Richardson and I. Walter. Wiley.

Acharya V. V., Johnson T.C. 2007. Insider trading in credit derivatives. Journal of Financial Economics 84:110–141.

Ait-Sahalia Y., Laeven R. J., Pelizzon L. 2014. Mutual excitation in eurozone sovereign CDS. Journal of Econometrics 183:151–167.

Allen F., Carletti E. 2006. Credit risk transfer and contagion. Journal of Monetary Economics 53:89–111.

Alter A., Beyer A. 2014. The dynamics of spillover effects during the European sovereign debt turmoil. Journal of Banking & Finance 42:134–153.

Alter A., Schuler Y. S. 2012. Credit spread interdependencies of European states and banks during the financial crisis. Journal of Banking & Finance 36:3444–3468.

Altman E., Rijken H. A. 2011. Toward a bottom-up approach to assessing sovereign default risk. Journal of Applied Corporate Finance 23:20–31.

Ammer J., Cai F. 2011. Sovereign CDS and bond pricing dynamics in emerging markets: Does the cheapest-to-deliver option matter? Journal of International Financial Markets, Institutions and Money 21:369–387.

Ang A., Longstaff F. A. 2013. Systemic sovereign credit risk: Lessons from the U.S. and Europe. Journal of Monetary Economics 60:493–510.

Arentsen E., Mauer D. C., Rosenlund B., Zhang H., Zhao F. 2015. Subprime mortgage defaults and credit default swaps. The Journal of Finance 70:689–731.

Arping S. 2014. Credit protection and lending relationships. Journal of Financial Stability 10:7–19. www.annualreviews.org Credit Default Swaps 21.

Ashcraft A. B., Santos J. A. 2009. Has the CDS market lowered the cost of corporate debt? Journal of Monetary Economics 56:514–523.

Augustin P. 2013. The term structure of CDS spreads and sovereign credit risk. Working Paper.

Augustin P. 2014. Sovereign credit default swap premia. Journal of Investment Management 12:65–102.

Augustin P., Boustanifar H., Breckenfelder J., Schnitzler J. 2015a. Sovereign to corporate risk spillovers. Working Paper.

Augustin P., Jiao F., Sarkissian S., Schill M. J. 2015b. Multi-market trading and cross-asset integration. Working Paper.

Augustin P., Subrahmanyam M. G., Tang D. Y., Wang S. Q. 2014. Credit default swaps: A survey. Foundations and Trends in Finance 9:1–196.

Augustin P., T´edongap R. 2015. Real economic shocks and sovereign credit risk. Journal of Financial and Quantitative Analysis Forthcoming.

Bai J., Wei S. J. 2014. When is there a strong transfer risk from the sovereigns to the corporates? Property rights gaps and CDS spreads. Working Paper.

Bedendo M., Cathcart L., El-Jahel L. 2015. Distressed debt restructuring in the presence of credit default swaps. Journal of Money, Credit and Banking Forthcoming.

Beirne J., Fratzscher M. 2013. The pricing of sovereign risk and contagion during the European sovereign debt crisis. Journal of International Money & Finance 34:60–82.

Benzoni L., Collin-Dufresne P., Goldstein R. S., Helwege J. 2015. Modeling credit contagion via the updating of fragile beliefs. Review of Financial Studies 28:1960–2008.

Berndt A., Jarrow R. A., Kang C. O. 2007. Restructuring risk in credit default swaps: An empirical analysis. Stochastic Processes and their Applications 117:1724–1749.

Biais B., Heider F., Hoerova M. 2015. Risk-sharing or risk-taking? Counterparty risk, incentives and margins. Journal of Finance Forthcoming.

Boehmer E., Chava S., Tookes H. E. 2015. Related securities and equity market quality: The case of CDS. Journal of Financial and Quantitative Analysis 50:509–541.

Bolton P., Oehmke M. 2011. Credit default swaps and the empty creditor problem. Review of Financial Studies 24:2617–2655.

Bruyckere V. D., Gerhardt M., Schepens G., Vennet R. V. 2013. Bank/sovereign risk spillovers in the European debt crisis. Journal of Banking & Finance 37:4793–4809.

Bulow J., Rogoff K. 1989. Sovereign debt: Is to forgive to forget? American Economic Review 79:43–50.

Campello M., Ladika T., Matta R. 2015. Debt restructuring costs and corporate bankruptcy: Evidence from CDS spreads. Working Paper.

Campello M., Matta R. 2013. Credit default swaps, firm financing and the economy. Working Paper.

Caporin M., Pelizzon L., Ravazzolo F., Rigobon R. 2013. Measuring sovereign contagion in Europe. NBER Working Paper 18741.

Chakraborty I., Chava S., Ganduri R. 2015. Credit default swaps and moral hazard in bank lending. Working Paper.

Che Y. K., Sethi R. 2014. Credit market speculation and the cost of capital. American Economic Journal: Microeconomics 1:1–34.

Chernov M., Schmid L., Schneider A. 2015. A macro finance view of US sovereign CDS premiums. Working Paper.

Colonnello S. 2013. Corporate governance and debt monitoring: The role of credit default swaps. Working Paper.

Danis A. 2013. Do empty creditors matter? Evidence from distressed exchange offers. Working Paper.

Danis A., Gamba A. 2014. The real effects of credit default swaps. Working Paper.

Darst M., Refayet E. 2015. The impact of CDS on firm financing and investment: Borrowing costs, spillovers, and default risk. Working Paper.

Das S. 1995. Credit risk derivatives. Journal of Derivatives 2:7–23.

Das S., Kalimipalli M., Nayak S. 2014. Did CDS trading improve the market for corporate bonds? Journal of Financial Economics 111:495–525.

Dieckmann S., Plank T. 2011. Default risk of advanced economies: An empirical analysis of credit default swaps during the financial crisis. Review of Finance 16:903–934.

Dockner E. J., Mayer M., Zechner J. 2013. Sovereign bond risk premiums. Working Paper.

Du L., Masli A., Meschke F. 2013. The effect of credit default swaps on the pricing of audit services. Working Paper.

Duffee G. R., Zhou C. 2001. Credit derivatives in banking: Useful tools for managing risk? Journal of Monetary Economics 48:25–54.

Duffie D. 1999. Credit swap valuation. Financial Analysts Journal 55:73–87.

Duffie D., Scheicher M., Vuillemey G. 2014. Central clearing and collateral demand. Journal of Financial Economics 116: 237–256.

Duffie D., Singleton K. J. 2003. Credit Risk: Pricing, Measurement and Management. Princeton University Press.

Eaton J., Gersovitz M. 1981. Debt with potential repudiation: Theoretical and empirical analysis. The Review of Economic Studies 48:289–309.

Ejsing J. W., Lemke W. 2011. The Janus-headed salvation: Sovereign and bank credit risk premia during 2008-09. Economics Letters 110:28–31.

Financial Crisis Inquiry Commission, United States of America. 2011. Final report of the National Commission on the causes of the financial and economic crisis in the United States. ISBN 978-0-16-087983-8.

Fostel A., Geanakoplos J. 2012. Tranching, CDS, and asset prices: How financial innovation can cause bubbles and crashes. American Economic Journal: Macroeconomics 4:190–225.

Fostel A., Geanakoplos J. 2015. Financial innovation, collateral and investment. Working Paper.

Fung H. G., Wen M. M., Zhang G. 2012. How does the use of credit default swaps affect firm risk and value? Evidence from US life and property/casualty insurance companies. Financial Management 41:979–1007.

Goderis B., Wagner W. 2011. Credit derivatives and sovereign debt crises. Working Paper.

Hakenes H., Schnabel I. 2010. Credit risk transfer and bank competition. Journal of Financial Intermediation 19:308–332.

Hebert B., Schreger J. 2015. The Costs of Sovereign Default: Evidence from Argentina. Working Paper.

Hilscher J., Pollet J. M., Wilson M. 2015. Are credit default swaps a sideshow? Evidence that information flows from equity to CDS markets. Journal of Financial and Quantitative Analysis 50:543–567.

Hirtle B. 2009. Credit derivatives and bank credit supply. Journal of Financial Intermediation 18:125–150.

Hortacsu A., Matvos G., Syverson C., Venkataraman S. 2013. Indirect costs of financial distress in durable goods industries: The case of auto manufacturers. Review of Financial Studies 26:1248–1290.

Hu H. T. C. 2015. Financial innovation and governance mechanisms: The evolution of decoupling and transparency. Business Lawyer 70.

Hu H. T. C, Black B. 2008. Debt, equity and hybrid decoupling: Governance and systemic risk implications. European Financial Management 14:663–709.

Ismailescu I., Phillips B. 2011. Savior or sinner? Credit default swaps and the market for sovereign debt. Working Paper. www.annualreviews.org Credit Default Swaps 23.

Jankowitsch R., Pullirsch R., Veza T. 2008. The delivery option in credit default swaps. Journal of Banking & Finance 32:1269–1285.

Jarrow R. A. 2011. The economics of credit default swaps. Annual Review of Financial Economics 3:235–257.

Jiang W., Zhu Z. 2015. Mutual fund holdings of credit default swaps: Liquidity management and risk taking. Working Paper.

Kallestrup R., Lando D., Murgoci A. 2014. Financial sector linkages and the dynamics of bank and sovereign credit spreads. Working Paper.

Karolyi S. A. 2013. Borrower risk-taking, CDS trading, and the empty creditor problem. Working Paper.

Kim G. H. 2013. Credit default swaps, strategic default, and the cost of corporate debt. Working Paper.

Kim J. B., Shroff P. K., Vyas D., Wittenberg-Moerman R. 2015. Active CDS trading and managers' voluntary disclosure. Working Paper.

La Porta R., de Silanes F. L., Shleifer A., Vishny R.W. 1998. Law and finance. Journal of Political Economy 106:1113–1155.

Lee J., Naranjo A., Sirmans S. 2015. Exodus from sovereign risk: Global asset and information networks in the pricing of corporate credit risk. Journal of Finance Forthcoming.

Lewis M. 2011. The big short. W. W. Norton & Company.

Li J. Y., Tang D. 2015. The leverage externalities of credit default swaps. Journal of Financial Economics Forthcoming.

Longstaff F. A., Pan J., Pedersen L. H., Singleton K. J. 2011. How sovereign is sovereign credit risk? American Economic Journal: Macroeconomics 3:75–103.

Loon Y. C., Zhong Z. K. 2014. The impact of central clearing on counterparty risk, liquidity, and trading: Evidence from the credit default swap market. Journal of Financial Economics 112:91–115.

Loon Y. C., Zhong Z. K. 2015. Does Dodd-Frank affect OTC transaction costs and liquidity? Evidence from real-time CDS trade reports. Journal of Financial Economics Forthcoming.

Lubben S. J., Narayanan R. P. 2012. CDS and the resolution of financial distress. Journal of Applied Corporate Finance 24:129–134.

Martin X., Roychowdhury S. 2015. Do financial market developments influence accounting practices? Credit default swaps and borrowers' reporting conservatism. Journal of Accounting and Economics 59:80–104.

Massa M., Zhang L. 2012. CDS and liquidity provision in the bond market. Working Paper.

Morgan Stanley. 2011. Sovereign CDS: Credit event and auction primer. Tech. rep., Morgan Stanley.

Morrison A. D. 2005. Credit derivatives, disintermediation, and investment decisions. The Journal of Business 78: 621–648.

Myers S. C. 1977. The determinants of corporate borrowing. Journal of Financial Economics 5:147–175.

Narayanan R., Uzmanoglu C. 2012. Public debt restructuring during crisis: Holdout vs. overhang. Working Paper.

Nashikkar A., Subrahmanyam M. G., Mahanti S. 2011. Liquidity and arbitrage in the market for credit risk. Journal of Financial and Quantitative Analysis 46:627–656.

Norden L., Buston C. S., Wagner W. 2014. Financial innovation and bank behavior: Evidence from credit markets. Journal of Economic Dynamics and Control 43:130–145.

Oehmke M., Zawadowski A. 2014. The anatomy of the CDS market. Working Paper.

Oehmke M., Zawadowski A. 2015. Synthetic or real? The equilibrium effects of credit default swaps on bond markets. Review of Financial Studies Forthcoming.

Pan J., Singleton K. J. 2008. Default and recovery implicit in the term structure of sovereign CDS spreads. The Journal of Finance 63:2345–2384.

Parlour C. A., Winton A. 2013. Laying off credit risk: Loan sales versus credit default swaps. Journal of Financial Economics 107:25–45.

Peristiani S., Savino V. 2011. Are credit default swaps associated with higher corporate defaults? Working Paper.

Portes R. 2010. Ban naked CDS. Euro Intelligence.

Remolona E., Scatigna M., Wu E. 2008. The dynamic pricing of sovereign risk in emerging markets: Fundamentals and risk aversion. Journal of Fixed Income 17:57–71.

Salomao J. 2014. Sovereign debt renegotiation and credit default swaps. Working Paper.

Saretto A., Tookes H. E. 2013. Corporate leverage, debt maturity, and credit supply: The role of credit default swaps. Review of Financial Studies 26:1190–1247.

Sgherri S., Zoli E. 2009. Euro area sovereign risk during the crisis. IMF Working Paper 09/222, International Monetary Fund.

Shan S. C., Tang D. Y., Winton A. 2014a. Do credit derivatives lower the value of creditor control rights? Evidence from debt covenants. Working Paper.

Shan S. C., Tang D. Y., Yan H. 2014b. Did CDS make banks riskier? The effects of credit default swaps on bank capital and lending. Working Paper.

Shim I., Zhu H. 2014. The impact of CDS trading on the bond market: Evidence from Asia. Journal of Banking & Finance 40:460–475.

Siriwardane E. 2015. Concentrated capital losses and the pricing of corporate credit risk. Working Paper.

Stephens E., Thompson J. R. 2014. CDS as insurance: Leaky lifeboats in stormy seas. Journal of Financial Intermediation 23:279–299.

Stulz R. M. 2010. Credit default swaps and the credit crisis. Journal of Economic Perspectives 24:73–92.

Subrahmanyam M. G., Tang D. Y., Wang S. Q. 2014. Does the tail wag the dog? The effect of credit default swaps on credit risk. Review of Financial Studies 27:2927–2960.

Subrahmanyam M. G., Tang D. Y., Wang S. Q. 2015. Credit default swaps, exacting creditors and corporate liquidity management. Working Paper.

Tett G. 2009. Fool's gold: How the bold dream of a small tribe at J.P. Morgan was corrupted by Wall Street greed and unleashed a catastrophe. Free Press.

Thompson J. R. 2010. Counterparty risk in financial contracts: Should the insured worry about the insurer? The Quarterly Journal of Economics 125:1195–1252.

Yorulmazer T. 2013. Has financial innovation made the world riskier? CDS, regulatory arbitrage and systemic risk. Working Paper.

10 Tools of Forward-Looking Management of Jobs in the Moroccan Ministry of Finance and Benchmark with Other Ministries

Malak Bouhazzama and Said Mssassi
University Abelmalek Essaadi, National School of Management, Tangier, Morocco

CONTENTS

10.1 INTRODUCTION

Human dimension remains especially deficient in terms of our public organizations[1], especially concerning the management of human resources, which constitutes one of the vulnerable points that characterizes the management of public organizations[2]. The present study is designed to further our understanding of two problems in the public administration:

- The nonexistence of an efficient practical methodology for developing and piloting competencies[3].
- The absence of objective criteria for the evaluation of personnel performances[4].

Studies and reports dedicated to the subject carried out under the public authority of the Ministry of the Modernization of Services noticed the following:

- A statutory and juridical traditional management.
- The inappropriateness of a budgeting frame founded on the principle of yearly basis.

10.2 PROPOSED METHODS

Any management is projected, to carry out the projected management is simply to reinforce this orientation, which attracts the ambition of management by highlighting certain choices. This requirement is obvious in the management of human resources of the Moroccan public administration, as in any organization. In effect, our choice of the Ministry of Finance is because of its role in piloting and implementing the strategy of administrative reform required by the Moroccan government. The program was carried out with the help of the World Bank, the European Union, and the African Development Bank. It is a strategy of reform of the public administration which aims at simplifying administrative structures, simplifying procedures, ameliorating performances, and raising the quality of benefits.

First of all, this subject was focused on the diagnosis of the tools of forward-looking management of jobs and skills implemented within the Ministry of Finance in order to take a little of height of view. Then, an exploratory qualitative study on a sample of 12 ministerial departments was necessary to be able to analyze the relationship between competences and performance across the various tools of the management of human resources. The objectives of this study are as follows:

- Identify, list, and analyze the tools of current forward-looking management of jobs and skills.
- Diagnose all the tools within the Ministry of Finance.
- Take stock of the actual progress of this system instituted since 2007.
- Put light on the central role across its tools in the development of performance.
- Undertake a benchmarking study at the ministerial department level.
- Perform a total analysis of the state of progress and the degrees according to the guide of the ministry of the modernization of services.
- Compare the actual situation of the Ministry of Finance in comparison with other departments.
- Get outside recommendations on the cause of weaknesses and raised faults hanging the analysis.

All in all, we cannot speak about system competitive forward-looking management of jobs and skills without discussing competitive tools. The valuation of these last would be the key to diagnosing the whole system[5], as well as to discover how it relates to performance within the public Moroccan administration. Basic tools that concern this study are as follows:

- Job and skill review that allows a classification of jobs and post offices of departments.

- Skill assessment is the analysis and the valuation of professional and personal competencies, as well as aptitude and motivation of a person. It leads to the definition of a realistic professional plan and can adapt to the job market, if needed, as well as highlight the need for continuing education.
- Questionnaire are valuable because they introduce numerous advantages, both for the colleague and his manager: recognition of performance and evolution of the career; help with the management of training and remunerations; and strategy and competitiveness of the firm[6].
- The Human Resources Information System: This is a software package of inserted management (PGI) or enterprise resources planning (ERP) that aims at regrouping several computer applications within a common system by taking care of the entire management of some or all functions of the organization, including accounting and financial management, human resources management, administrative, logistics management, and so on[7].

So, a diagnosis of the actual situation of those tools proves to be necessary, but this valuation cannot be efficient if it is not balanced by the level of total performance in the public administration, which that encouraged use to carry out a benchmark study while adopting a qualitative approach[8] on a sample of 12 ministerial departments through a deep and individual semi-structured interview. It contains 16 questions grouped into five parties.

The first party (two questions) allows an understanding of the environment better by being progressively focused on the function of human resources and to find with link between the percentage of the personnel and tools worked out within the ministry. Three other following parties (eight questions) approach the heart of our problem by assessing the tools by shining a light on the strong points and weaknesses of the four fundamental tools. Finally, the last party, which concerns performance will allow to answer our problems by clarifying, on one hand, the relation between the tools of GPEC and performance in the public administration and, on the other hand, two ubiquitous approaches in public administration: classical administration and modern administration based on competencies.

10.3   RESULTS

Sixteen interviews were carried out among the 12 ministries. For the Ministry of Economy and Finance, it should be noted that six interviews were accomplished:

- Four at the level of the Directorate of General and Administrative Affairs.
- An interview at the public domain level.
- An interview at the level of the Administration of Customs and Indirect Taxes.

As for the sample, we chose to question three types of civil servants:

- The leader of division of Human Resource who carries out strategy as well as policies of the ministry.

- The section head, who represents the intermediate supervision and links between the director and servants of service.

The frame manager operating in forward-looking management of jobs and skills, with a direct contact with other servants and accomplished one or some of the tools. This panel is the most heterogeneous possible to allow us to compare their points of view and to determine differences, if need be. We were confronted with a difficulty in questioning leaders of the division:

- 61.53% of the public servants loaded with the management of human resources are in general young dynamics, endowed with an opening of mind and that accept change easily (behavior of change).
- 56.25% are females.
- 80% have the ladder 11, which reflects a very good intellectual level and a highly analytical mind, which is the result of solid training and years of experience very developed mind of analysis is further to years of experience or thanks to a very solid training.

For the seniority, it varies from 0 to 21 years which shows that number of years of experience is not a fundamental criterion in the philosophy of the forward-looking management of jobs and skills. Discussions in general lasted between one hour and one and a half hours and were sufficient for collecting the necessary information. It is necessary to note, for instance, that it was difficult to supervise two leaders. In both cases, discussions were, however, very rich and extended, as in the plan of our guide, and every interview took place following the plan, but seven topics were favored:

- Forward-looking management of jobs and skills in the public service.
- The strong points and weaknesses of tools.
- The degree of taking over of tools.
- Definition of the performance of the human resource management in public service.
- Criteria of valuation of the performance of this function.
- Measure of performance RH by tools.
- Reconciliation between the classical administration and the modern one.

10.4 CONCLUSION

The Ministry of Finances and Privatization has been working for several years to modernize its modes of management and the systems of information. The plan of forward-looking management of jobs and skills was begun for an overhaul of the function of human resources. In effect, the process which was implemented had an objective to develop the public service and to provide a model where competencies will have only the master word to attain performance. However, the presence of a classical system based on hierarchy slows down this change.

It is necessary to use the moral and factual authority that comes with a political and administrative leading role. It will be necessary to know how to ask these leaders to get involved and to know how to make their involvement easier. It will be necessary to envisage when and how their involvement will be necessary and give them all the information they need, as well as instruments necessary for their interventions.

It is necessary to know how to gather together all aspects of forward-looking management of jobs and skills. This demands good records, to communicate with transparency, and to link people to the development of these records. It is necessary to communicate to keep the momentum of reform and preserve the membership of the actors. It is necessary to allow all actors to follow in a collegiate way the evolution of the records. In terms of a cultural plan, it is necessary to create a consistent speech on change and try to broadcast it in all areas of the administration.

Changes have to remain rather simple, easy to establish, and concrete in the eyes of the actors of the administration. It will be necessary to envisage support (tools and training) with this effect. You will not have to try to advance too fast, but with regularity and determination.

The members will want to optimize the contribution of the ERP so as to give information on changes that are standard and examples on desired practices. Human Resources Database will be available for consultation at any time, almost everywhere and allows providing information standards and consistent answers to users.

The communication at all levels of the organization will be the key to success. It will be necessary to explain simply and in concrete terms the perspective of and justification for changes. A strategy of communication is essential.

The strategy of communication will contribute to acknowledge the innovative organizations so it won't be a question of identifying who are the "champions," but who play a key role to serve the public administration.

REFERENCES

1. Diverez J, "Politiques et techniques de direction du personnel", Paris, EME (1970).
2. Fombonne J, "Historique de la fonction ressources humaines – Des prémices de l'administration au management des ressources humaines", Paris, Organisation (2009).
3. Simon Ha, "Strategy and organizational evolution", Strategic Management journal, (1993).
4. Weiss D, "Nouvelles formes d'entreprise et relations de travail", Revue Française de Gestion, Mars (1994).
5. Igalens J, "Audit des ressources humaines", Paris, Liaisons, Option gestion, 2ème edition (1994).
6. Mallet L, "La Gestion Prévisionnelle de l'emploi", Paris, Edition Liaisons, Collection Gestion (1992).
7. Françoise Kerlan, "Guide de la gestion prévisionnelle des emplois et des compétences", Editions Eyrolles (2004).
8. Eric Vernette, "Techniques d'étude de marché", librairie Vuibert (2000).

11 Artificial Intelligence– Based Methods of Financial Time Series for Trading Experts in a Relational Database to Generate Decisions

Khalid Abouloula[1], Ali Ou-yassine[1],
Salah-ddine Krit[1], and Mohamed Elhoseny[2]
[1] Ibn Zohr University, Agadir, Morocco
[2] Mansoura University, Dakahlia, Egypt

CONTENTS

11.1 INTRODUCTION

The philosophy of automated trading encouraged serious individual traders to step into the world of professional institutions, as the automated trading platform provided professional tools that are completely similar to what traders can use at banks, financial institutions or brokers [1]. In manual trading, there are limitations; one of the first limitations is that execution performance will be slow, so there is a server between the trader and the execution (the broker), so it is not consistent access to the market. Today, we have algorithmic trading, high-frequency trading, and direct market access (DMA), which means that it is possible to directly access the market without an intermediary and trade directly [2]. Nowadays, most digital information is stored on servers. All these servers are connected to a few networks. This system has existed for some time now. Problems were detected but never resolved, mostly for technological reasons. Indeed, we can talk about the security or the stability of these servers. At present, if the server we are connected to is crashing, we will not be able to do anything, and we will have to wait for the server to be put back into service in order to access our data. It has happened to us all at one time or another that a web site does not work or that a device does not connect. This is due to our current system that is server-based, and this is the classic problem in the world of finance, because it is necessary at the end of the day to make the settlement between the banks [3]. All this could disappear if Blockchain technology is adopted.

Currently, several approaches have been proposed in the world, some already in experimentation. The most notable approaches are based primarily on a peer-to-peer (P2P) network to manage the distribution without the use of Blockchain. All these solutions mainly address the issue of transaction security [4]. The solutions based on Blockchain are few, and the closest one to our approach that uses a Moroccan digital currency remains that of Bitcoin. This cryptocurrency allows individual traders to trade currency anywhere in the world in a short time and at a very low cost. This paper presents a view of the various applications of this technology, which is now the focus of attention of all countries in the world to facilitate trading in all international markets [5], and the current understanding of Blockchain technology and how to participate in reducing the cost of digital currency conversion to trading between customers and individual traders. We provide a study on the various opportunities for sustainability associated with the use of Blockchain technology through which it occurs. This study will help novice traders and researchers continue to assess the potential use of Blockchain technology to improve durability. However, before looking at Blockchain technology in the financial markets and how it can reduce the cost of order transfer, we first identify the concept of a trading broker and how the platform to the server is slow to make decisions. And we will propose a code of the digital currency developed in the C++ language, which we will use in the application of the Blockchain technique.

11.2   THE CONCEPT OF THE BROKER IN TRADING

A stockbroker is also called a registered representative or financial advisor or simply an intermediary, and this is a professional who executes sales and purchases orders and other securities on the stock market, or even outside the stock exchange for a commission or fee. Brokerage companies and transactions for retail and institutional clients and brokerage companies and brokerage dealers are also referred to as brokers. It was usual that only the wealthy would be able to hire a broker to get to the stock market [6]. Many speculators feel puzzled when opening a real account for them from the large number of companies in the market, but the decision to open an account with the companies of the bank needs to trializing, thinking and discussing, and the time spent in the search will give a good idea of the services of the company and the fees charged by the company for these services. Most brokerage companies offer mini accounts and micro accounts, which are very small accounts where the pips reach a cent, and to open an account with them starts from $200.

11.2.1   ELECTRONIC TRADING

Successful trading in the Forex market requires a commitment to a set of rules and principles that will make a major difference in the results of private trading. In the past few years, the Forex market has spread significantly throughout the world, especially the Arab world, due to the development of information and communication technology. It became clear that the most important reason for the failure of the Forex market, which eventually led to the loss of money for many traders and left them trading in foreign currency without return, is random trading disorder [7]. In addition, most traders in the Forex market were trading without having any prior experience or without following the rules and principles of sound trading that would have brought them success. The most important rules that will lead to high levels of profits when trading in the Forex market are explained next.

11.2.1.1   Open a Trading Account

The beginning of trading in the currency market through a fake trading account or a demo account is one of the fundamentals of trading in the currency market. Starting with a virtual trading account helps to evaluate the trading platform of the selected broker, by trading through the imaginary account through fake funds and not real money. There are several basic considerations for choosing a trading platform because this platform is the program that will carry out all your trading periods and will analyse your trades [8]. The trading platform must be easy in terms of characteristics and understanding in terms of simplicity and ease of use, in addition to the speed of implementation of all purchase orders and sale and stop loss orders and objectives in the trading program. The trading platform should contain analysis tools, charts, and recent data on the trading market and should include all the latest news related to the trading market.

11.2.1.2 Currency Pair to Trade

Any currency for any country can be traded, but this is dependent on the brokerage company through which it enters into the currency market for each country of its own currency. In the Forex market, each currency is given a special code so it can be dealt with without mistakes. For example, several countries may be similar in the name of the currency you are dealing with. The dollar is the name of the currency of the United States of America, the currency of Australia, and the currency of Canada and many other countries, so when there are mistakes in buying and selling, it was agreed internationally that the currency of each country be given a symbol of its own known throughout the world. These codes are known as ISO codes [9], as shown in Figure 11.1.

11.2.2 Graphical User Trading

A trading platform is a type of software that acts as a link between the trader and the brokerage company. This platform displays some information such as currency exchange rates and charts. It contains an interface to enter trading orders for the brokerage firm to execute. The platform software is based on the type of computer, meaning that the application is installed on the personal computer of the trader, who is running a computer in one of the operating systems.

All brokerage companies now allow online trading on the Internet with ease, but the difference between one company and another is their trading program. Is it a complex or easy-to-use trading program? Most brokerage companies have two programs: Java program or Web and the program that can be loaded on machine. And often the downloaded trading program on machine who works faster does not work on all operating systems, for example, a program that work on windows

Currency Pair	Countries	FX Geek Speak
EUR/USD	Euro zone / United States	"euro dollar"
USD/JPY	United States / Japan	"dollar yen"
GBP/USD	United Kingdom / United States	"pound dollar"
USD/CHF	United States / Switzerland	"dollar swissy"
USD/CAD	United States / Canada	"dollar loonie"
AUD/USD	Australia / United States	"aussie dollar"
NZD/USD	New Zealand / United States	"kiwi dollar"

FIGURE 11.1   The currency pairs.

do not work on the Mac and the program that work on the Mac and forced to work on the web application, it will work on any computer. Most of the trading programs that work on Java are more secure than the programs that you download on your computer in terms of securing implementation and data transfer [10]. Working in Forex needs a high-speed Internet connection; slow Internet trading ensures that you will not experience fast service and fast execution. Operations are done in less than a second, so you need fast Internet access to ensure that the operations are done quickly.

11.2.3 SPREADS

Spread is the difference between the selling price and the purchase price. You must check carefully the selling and buying teams in the currencies offered by the company because many speculators ignore this, but it is very important. For example, if GBP/USD pair has five pips, that will calculate in a day of trading, in an open and close of the trades at the same day, that mean at everyday a single transaction in every time traders buy or sell GBP/USD, they pays five points from the account. The price of the point depends on the value of the contract. Imagine, for example, that the point is worth $10. That means that the $50 deducted in each transaction, unfortunately, performs 15 transactions per month. As a simple matter, you can know that you lose 75 points in a month and, of course, each point of 75 stops, according to contract value $1, $10, or even $100. However, why pay spread while it is possible to make it profit. For this reason, it has become essential to eliminate the intermediary companies because the spreads are larger, the losses are greater [11].

11.2.4 INFRASTRUCTURE FOR CURRENT MARKET

Network topology is defined as the structure by which nodes and network connections are connected. We mean both networks: a computer network and a biological network. In terms of computer network typology, it refers specifically to the logical or physical topology of the network. We will learn more about networking topology [12].

11.2.4.1 Types of Network Topology

There are many major types of network topologies (Figure 11.2) that are divided into two parts: the first one is more abstract, the second is more stratified and multispecies and from it we have following types of topologies:

  a. *Bus Topology*
     This is the type of network topology in which each network node connects to a shared transmission medium, which only has two parties, often called the backbone or trunk; all the data exchanged by the network elements pass through it and can be received from all nodes at one time, ignoring generation delays.
  b. *Star Topology*
     In local area network (LAN), using this topology, all machines are connected to a hub. In contrast to linear topology, each machine can communicate with

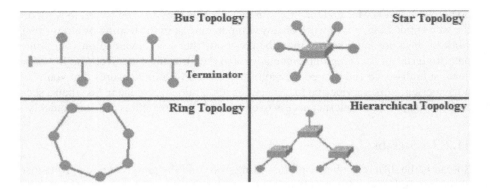

FIGURE 11.2 The physical structures of the network.

the central axis point to point. All signals pass through the central axis acting as a booster or repeater of the signal, allowing the signal to reach a greater distance. In this structure, each computer has a direct link to the hub.

c. *Ring Topology*

In the design of a ring-type network, the devices are connected to the network with a continuous loop or a circuit of the wire. The signals move around the loop in one direction and pass through each device on the network. Each computer on the network acts as a repeater. The signal is reactived and reinforced then sent on the network to the following computer, so when the signal is sent to each peripheral of the network then the failure of only one device will stop the operation of network.

d. *Hierarchical Topology*

This is known as the central control of the central computer on the computers of the terminal, which contains only a screen and keyboard keys that are used to enter orders and cannot be stored and processed only through the central computer host. It is a redundant algorithm for the creation of networks that can reproduce the unique characteristics of a nonstandard network topology and provide high contract aggregation at the same time.

It is noted that each of the previous types of networks of different structural and engineering design has its advantages and disadvantages, but the second type, that is, the star network, is the best of these types because of its simplicity and ease of design. In this type, there is a possibility of detecting an error quickly and easily and the possibility of future expansion of the network flexibly.

11.2.4.2 Logical Topology

Logical topology is the way a signal behaves between network nodes, or the way data travel from one device to another in the network, regardless of the physical interface. A logical topology does not necessarily have to be analogous to a physical topology; for example:

- In Ethernet networks that use twisted pair, they follow a logical linear topology with the appearance of a physical linear topology.
- In IBM's Token Ring networks, it follows an orbital logical pathology with the appearance of an astrophysical topology.

The logical topology expresses the shape of the path that the data take between the nodes of the grid, while expressing the true path of the signals (optical, electronic) when they cross the nodes.

11.3 CRYPTOCURRENCIES AND BLOCKCHAIN

Blockchain is the core technology of Bitcoin, as it represents proof and documentation of all transactions on the Web. This technique is suitable for all types of financial transactions, including services, commodities, and others. Its potential is almost unlimited, from raising taxes to enabling immigrants to send money to their families living in countries experiencing difficulties in banking.

The global market has become very dynamic at present, in part because of the emergence of many technologies daily such as artificial intelligence, large data, and Internet of things that can change our entire lifestyle. Blockchain is one of the technologies that can have the same impact on our lives, especially in the financial and information technology fields. More people are seeing the potential of this technology, and terms such as Bitcoin and digital currencies are becoming common [13].

Of course, marketers who usually ask about the impact of any new technology on them can ask about the effect of Blockchain on the long-term marketing industry. The first is how Blockchain affects the basic technology used in commission marketing; the second aspect is how to apply commission marketing based on coding and Blockchain technology.

11.3.1 CRYPTOCURRENCIES

Cryptocurrency started when an anonymous person named Satoshi Nakamoto invented Bitcoin in 2008, an open-source encrypted currency that can be used for P2P trading. This currency initially found interest from a small community of coding professionals and programers, but soon spread among ordinary people.

In order to understand how big a change in people's dealings with Bitcoin can be compared to a situation of the currency in 2009 when one of the coding professionals tried to sell 10,000 homes for $50 without finding a buyer; while the value of one Bitcoin recently is 1,000 dollars, and indeed, the people who have ventured into buying thousands of Bitcoin at the start are millionaires now [14]. Because the Bitcoin market is becoming increasingly saturated, many alternative electronic currencies have appeared to be unevenly successful, and buyers of these currencies often have the wrong hope of replicating the financial success of the Bitcoin pioneers.

Coded currencies are guaranteed by trust, security, confidentiality, and the benefit of reducing the fees for financial transactions that mandatory money and banks are unable to provide today. While traditional remittances require at least three days, the Bitcoin transactions take place within an hour or less. While remittance charges in traditional institutions such as Western Union amount to 10% of the value of the remittances, the Bitcoin remittances charge less than 1%.

There is a limited and final number of Bitcoin, which is 21 million, which makes it a shrinkage currency whose price is determined by the law of supply and demand, whereas central banks can control the prices of paper money by printing more money. Encrypted currency users do not need to trust a third party during the conversion of these currencies or exchange of data, since there is no central unit to control them, but thousands of distributed nodes maintain the integrity of the general record of encrypted currencies, or the so-called Blockchain, which hinders any attempt to modify previously installed transactions [15].

11.3.2 THE CURRENCY OF BITCOIN

The currency of Bitcoin is like any currency, in that in order to have value there must be a limited number of them. Bitcoin is produced during a process called Bitcoin Mining, a process in which people who use the power of their computers to encrypt certain data on the Bitcoin are rewarded. This means that coded currencies are a by-product of a much more revolutionary technique of Blockchain [16].

Blockchain has a large role in organizing transactions for its customers on the Internet, which is based on a series of blocks that help to save the information of each digital wallet and know its own account and cannot be found on any other account because the insurance of the accounts is to have a private key in the network. Every time a sum of Bitcoin is spent, it is called a transaction and has a private key. With this key, the customer can withdraw the amount from his account.

A transaction is a process in sequential blocks with an encrypted signature, where signatures can be matched by views or by covering the keys, it is a private key. Therefore the stealing of data or accounts is only through customer's path. Blockchain is a great network that does not allow suspicious operations [17].

11.3.3 MARKETING WITH BLOCKCHAIN AND CRYPTOCURRENCIES

Blockchain and cryptocurrencies have been successful and growing over the past few years, so the present may be the best time to enter Blockchain-based commission marketing, where the market is still unsaturated. In this case, you can join one of the commission marketing programs and invite others and get a percentage of the profits or get a specific amount of encrypted digital currency for it.

However, such things are not entirely clear, as the encoded digital currency market is very volatile, and the values of the most stable currencies such as Bitcoin can fluctuate dramatically from month to month. In addition, there are very few commissions based on Blockchain and cryptocurrencies, so joining such programs requires advanced knowledge of such programs and can cause a financial disaster, at worst, if the program or currency is supported by insensitive people [18].

Beyond exchange rate fluctuations that affect profit and loss, there are other benefits and risks to consider before trading with foreign currencies in composition and other digital currencies.

11.3.3.1   Decentralized Assessments

One of the most important features of Forex trading with Bitcoin is that there is no central bank to assess the indiscriminate change of developers. Due to its decentralized nature, the prices of Bitcoin are free of geopolitical influence, as well as macroeconomic issues such as inflation or interest rates [19].

11.3.3.2   Leverage

Most Forex brokers offer a high leverage of up to 1/1000. Experienced traders can use this to their advantage. However, these high margins should be treated with extreme caution, as they may further amplify the potential loss.

11.3.3.3   Process Cost

All transactions are digitally signed on public networks without interference from banks or agencies. Consequently, there are usually no costs or commissions on these transactions, even for global transfers. This improves your business profits.

11.3.3.4   Cost Reduction by Intermediaries

Most foreign exchange brokers that accept cryptocurrency reduce brokerage fees and spread costs to attract new trading clients.

11.3.3.5   Security

Bitcoin transactions do not need you to disclose your bank account details or credit card details to deposit or withdraw funds, especially when dealing with foreign intermediaries.

11.3.3.6   No Geographic Boundaries

The circulation of digital currencies, especially Bitcoin, eliminated global borders and the problem of currency trading within the same geographical framework. For example, a trader in Africa can trade any foreign exchange through an intermediary based in the United Kingdom.

Historically, the application of transactions was based on norms and traditions until the emergence of religions which began with treaties, then the enactment of laws for this effect. However, the manipulation of these laws burdened the world of transactions, and it has become necessary to search for new ways to reduce this absurdity especially in the time of the technological revolution, where the world turned to the code instead of the laws.

11.3.4   Blockchain Technology

Blockchain has experienced continuous growth because each time a block is completed, a new block is created. The blocks are connected to each other in correct chronological order so that each block contains the former block. On each computer connected to the Bitcoin network followed by a client that checks and tracks transactions, there is a copy of the Blockchain, which is automatically loaded when you join the Bitcoin network. The full version of Blockchain contains logs for each transaction executed without exception.

11.3.4.1 Hash of Current Block

A hash function takes a few data segments and returns a constant string of bits called the hash value of encryption, so that any change in the original data will result in a significant change in the hash value of encryption. The encrypted data is usually called the message, and the amount of encryption encoded is called the digest. Examples of the hash's encryption function include the algorithms MD5, SHA1, and SHA256, as shown in Figure 11.3.

Thus, in order to add a new block to the block chain, the nodes participating in the creation of the chain must launch a cryptographic process, which is the calculation of the hash of the block. The purpose of this method is to convert data into a pseudorandom sequence of digits. It is impossible to modify the input data of the algorithm to obtain a precise result. This is due to the random nature of the algorithm.

A hash has many applications in the field of information security, especially in digital signatures, message authentication codes, and other types of authentication to discover duplicate information or entity files, For example:

```
static const word32 SHA256_K[64] = {
0x428a2f98, 0x71374491, 0xb5c0fbcf, 0xe9b5dba5,
0x3956c25b, 0x59f111f1, 0x923f82a4, 0xab1c5ed5,
0xd807aa98,0x12835b01, 0x243185be, 0x550c7dc3,
0x72be5d74, 0x80deb1fe, 0x9bdc06a7, 0xc19bf174,
0xe49b69c1, 0xefbe4786, 0x0fc19dc6, 0x240ca1cc,
0x2de92c6f, 0x4a7484aa, 0x5cb0a9dc, 0x76f988da,
0x983e5152, 0xa831c66d, 0xb00327c8, 0xbf597fc7,
0xc6e00bf3,0xd5a79147, 0x06ca6351, 0x14292967,
0x27b70a85,0x2e1b2138, 0x4d2c6dfc, 0x53380d13,
0x650a7354,0x766a0abb, 0x81c2c92e, 0x92722c85,
0xa2bfe8a1, 0xa81a664b, 0xc24b8b70, 0xc76c51a3,
0xd192e819,0xd6990624, 0xf40e3585, 0x106aa070,
0x19a4c116,0x1e376c08, 0x2748774c, 0x34b0bcb5,
0x391c0cb3, 0x4ed8aa4a, 0x5b9cca4f, 0x682e6ff3,
0x748f82ee, 0x78a5636f, 0x84c87814, 0x8cc70208,
0x90befffa, 0xa4506ceb, 0xbef9a3f7, 0xc67178f2
}
```

11.3.4.2 Hash of the Previous Block

The hash of the previous block is the third element of the block (Figure 11.4). This effectively creates a series of connected blocks and this makes Blockchain safe. If we have a series of three blocks, each block has the unique number hash and the hash of the previous block, so when block 3 indicates block 2 and block 2 indicates block 1, where block 1 is different because it is not possible to refer to an earlier block because it is simply the block that was first created, the block is called the origin or composition.

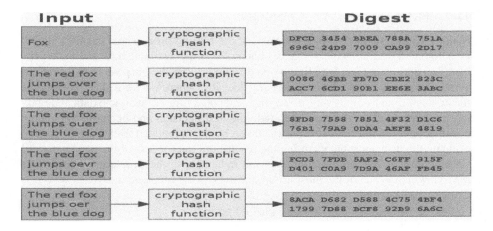

FIGURE 11.3   The hash function SHA1.

If the second block is tampered with, this will change the hash value of the block, so this will make the third block and all subsequent blocks incorrect because they no longer store the correct number of the previous block. Any change in the contents of the blocks will make all the subsequent blocks incorrect and unacceptable. However, the encryption technology is not enough to prevent tampering with information, because computers these days are very fast and can recalculate thousands of hashes in seconds. Actually, it is possible to manipulate the block and recalculate the new hash to the following blocks to make Blockchain true again and connected; to avoid the possibility of this manipulation, the string of blocks has something else to prevent it called the proof of work.

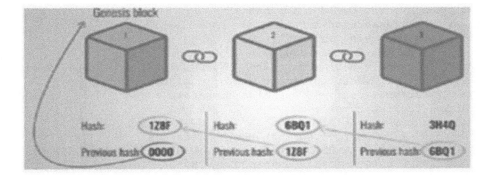

FIGURE 11.4   The genesis blocks.

11.4 PROCESS AND DISCUSSIONS

Making successful decisions is the basis of the trading process and has high profits by automated trading, which arranges and collects the available data and makes the best decision. Automated trading worked to determine the purpose of the decision and the basic priorities when making any decision; where we were able to overcome the crisis of time by analyzing, arranging, and collecting the available data and making the best use of it, the machine made the best decision and began to implement it immediately. After the decision was taken by the automated trader, we worked to evaluate the decisions and examine the results and the success of the decision, until we found a way to integrate four common indicators in the simple moving average (SMA), which is one of the most used indicators in the financial markets.

Code of SMA trend

double SMA (const int position, const int period,

const double & price [])

```
{
double result=0.0;
if (position>=period-1 && period>0)
{for (int i =0 ; I < period ; i++)
result+=price[position-i];
result/=period;
}
Return (result);
}
```

With that, we were able to make the right decision at the right time; we also didn't stop there, we went even further, while we studied all trades covered by traders when they are forced to trade via brokers who cost traders more than 10%. While there is a modern and safe technology known as Blockchain technology, from this study we present the following:

Genesis block

```
char* pszTimestamp = "The Times 03/Jan/2009 Chancellor on
brink of second bailout for banks";
        CTransaction txNew;
        txNew.vin.resize(1);
        txNew.vout.resize(1);
        txNew.vin[0].scriptSig     = CScript() << 486604799 <<
CBigNum(4) << vector<unsigned char>((unsigned char*)
pszTimestamp, (unsigned char*)pszTimestamp +
strlen(pszTimestamp));
        txNew.vout[0].nValue      = 50 * COIN;
        txNew.vout[0].scriptPubKey = CScript() <<
CBigNum("0x5F1DF16B2B704C8A578D0BBAF74D385CDE12C11EE50455F3C43
8EF4C3FBCF649B6DE611FEAE06279A60939E028A8D65C10B73071A6F167192
74855FEB0FD8A6704") << OP_CHECKSIG;
        CBlock block;
        block.vtx.push_back(txNew);
```

```
        block.hashPrevBlock = 0;
        block.hashMerkleRoot = block.BuildMerkleTree();
        block.nVersion = 1;
        block.nTime    = 1231006505;
        block.nBits    = 0x1d00ffff;
        block.nNonce   = 2083236893;
    }
      return true;
}
```

When we change a value here, the genesis block gets a different hash and the result is a different Blockchain that will not connect to wallets. Now, to see what happens when new blocks are created, a copy of those blocks is distributed to the node in the network and each node is sure that the block has not been manipulated, then it is combined into the standard string for each node. All nodes in the network "vote" on which blocks are sound and which are unsound. The blocks that are manipulated will be rejected from the rest of the nodes in the network. Blockchain must manipulate all the blocks in the string and reproduce the proof of work for each block and control more than 50% of the network. Only then will the manipulated blocks be acceptable to everyone, and this is impossible to do.

11.5 CONCLUSIONS

The trend toward decentralized renewable energy has increased; the Blockchain technique can be used to ensure that the purchase and sale of electricity is error-free and that each household gets the right amount of energy it produces, a process that requires a lot of automation to avoid bureaucracy. Smart is perfect in this case. Blockchain can also be used in many other areas such as fraud detection, anti-money laundering, and data management, as well as commission marketing.

Authorities should not see these new technologies as threats, but rather as useful technologies in one way or another. For that, the administration must pass to the digital revolution by dematerializing. But beforehand, it would have to be recognized in the legal texts by government as profitable, whatever the asset which is registered there.

REFERENCES

[1] Abouloula, K., Brahim, E. L. H., Krit, S. D., 2018. Money management limits to trade by robot trader for automatic trading. International Journal of Engineering, Science and Mathematics, 7(3), 195–206.
[2] Abouloula, K., Brahim, E. L. H., Krit, S. D. Using a Robot Trader for Automatic Trading International Conference on Engineering & MIS 2018, Altınbaş University, Istanbul, Turkey, June 19–21, 2018.
[3] Khan, M., Khan, S., Elhoseny, M., Syed Hassan, A., Sung Wook, B., 2019. Efficient fire detection for uncertain surveillance environment. IEEE Transactions on Industrial Informatics.
[4] Elhoseny, M., Hassanien, A., Dynamic Wireless Sensor Networks: New Directions for Smart Technologies, Published in Studies in Systems, Decision and Control by Springer, (DOI: 10.1007/978-3-319-92807-4).

[5] Metawa, N., Elhoseny, M., Hassanien, A., Hassan, K., 2019. Expert Systems in Finance: Smart Financial Applications in Big Data Environments, 1st Edition, Taylor & Francis, Milton Park, Milton.

[6] Murphy, J., 1999. Technical Analysis of the Financial Markets: A Comprehensive Guide to Trading Methods and Applications, 2nd Edition, New York Institute of Finance, New York [u.a.].

[7] Hassanien, A. E., Elhoseny, M., Cybersecurity and Secure Information Systems: Challenges and Solutions in Smart Environments, Published in Advanced Sciences and Technologies for Security Applications by Springer.

[8] Abouloula, K., Krit, S. D. Pattern to Build a Robust Trend Indicator for Automated Trading (https://www.routledge.com/Expert-Systems-in-Finance-Smart-Financial-Applications-in-Big-Data-Environments/Metawa-Elhoseny-Hassanien-Hassan/p/book/9780367109523)

[9] Müller, U. A., Dacorogna, M. M., Olsen, R. B., Pictet, O. V., Schworz, M., Morgenegg, C., 1990. Statistical study of foreign exchange rates, empirical evidence of price change law and intraday analysis. Journal of Banking and Finance, 14, 1189–1208.

[10] Kirilenko, A. A., Lo, A. W., 2013. Moore's law versus Murphy's law: Algorithmic trading and its discontents. Journal of Economic Perspectives, 27(2), 51–72.

[11] Athey, S., 2017. Beyond prediction: Using big data for policy problems. Science, 355(6324), 483–485.

[12] Lee, C., Mucklow, B., Ready, M., 1993. Spreads, depths, and the impact of earnings information: An intraday analysis. The Review of Financial Studies, 6(2), 345–374.

[13] Deng, Justin, Wu, Siheng, Sun, Kenny, Comparison of RIP, OSPF and EIGRP Routing Protocols based on OPNET, ENSC 427: Communication Networks Spring 2014.

[14] Blumberg, J., We Need to Shut Bitcoin and All Other Cryptocurrencies Down. Here's Why, March 2018. (https://www.forbes.com/sites/jasonbloomberg/2018/03/10/we-need-to-shut-bitcoin-and-all-other-cryptocurrencies-down-hereswhy/#1dbed32b1bca)

[15] Bollen, R., 2013. The legal status of online currencies: Are bitcoins the future. Journal of Banking and Finance Law and Practice, 38 (electronically available http://ssrn.com:80/abstract=2285247)

[16] FATF, Virtual Currencies – Key Definitions and Potential AML/CFT Risks, June 2014. (http://www.fatf-gafi.org/media/fatf/documents/reports/Virtual-currency-key-definitions-and-potential-aml-cft-risks.pdf, 7)

[17] Kaplanov, N. M., 2012. Nerdy money: Bitcoin, the private digital currency, and the case against its regulation. Temple Law Review, 46 (electronically available via https://papers.ssrn.com/sol3/papers.cfm?abstract_id=2115203)

[18] Bratspies, R. M., Cryptocurrencies and the Myth of the Trustless Transaction, March 2018, 49 (electronically available via https://ssrn.com/abstract=3141605)

[19] Ølnes, S., Ubacht, J., Janssen, M., 2017. Blockchain in government: Benefits and implications of distributed ledger technology for information sharing. Government Information Quarterly, 34, 355–364.

12 Modeling Energy Consumption of Freight Vehicles with MLR

Ech-Chelfi Wiame and El Hammoumi Mohammed
Sidi Mohammed Ben Abdellah University (USMBA),
Fez, Morocco

CONTENTS

Table of Abbreviations:

SCM	Supply chain management
RFT	Road freight transport
CO$_2$	Carbon dioxide
FP	Fiscal power
GVWR	Gross vehicle weight rating
EW	Empty weight
ρ	Coefficient of Pearson
γ	Acceleration (m^2/s)
Vn	Vehicle n
Vmax	Maximum speed
Yi	Energy consumption (L/100 km) according to the model i

12.1 INTRODUCTION

In the last century, there has been a dramatic increase in economic activity around the world. One of the side effects of this is the increase in the use of transport modes and consequently the increase in CO$_2$ emissions.

The uncontrolled and poorly planned growth of freight transport has led to several problems such as road congestion, environmental pollution, and the deterioration of

115

public health [1]. So, CO_2 emissions are related not only to the distance traveled by the vehicle but also to the characteristics of vehicles, driver behavior on the road, strategic choices of the company, infrastructure, etc. According to the literature, fuel consumption and CO_2 emissions are strictly interconnected. However, this relationship is not applicable to other air pollutants, such as particulate matter, NOx, and CO [2, 3].

This chapter classifies the factors of fuel consumption on three levels (macroscopic, mesoscopic, and microscopic). Each level is modeled by a multiple regression function to measure the impact of each factor and reformulate the general prediction function.

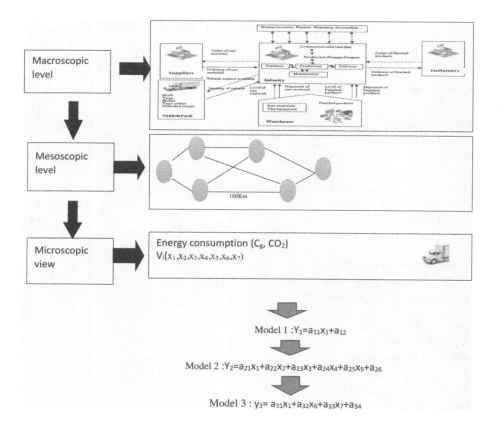

Vehicle energy consumption $Y_i = \sum a_{ij} x_k$ is a multivariable function influenced by internal factors related to the characteristics of vehicles (GVWR, EW, FP, age, etc.) and external factors related to the driver, speed, infrastructure, climate, etc.

The prediction of CO_2 emissions has become an important research area, as it would provide clues and raise awareness of environmental stability.

Emissions of gaseous elements such as CO_2 are becoming a global concern as greenhouse gases have the greatest impact on environmental problems.

Nevertheless, choosing the right methods to predict CO_2 emissions depends on a wide range of factors that involve both qualitative and quantitative variables.

12.2   THE DATA COLLECTION

A fleet of 74 vehicles of different categories was studied for one year with 56 different drivers. The company in question is an innovative olive oil industrial company in the Moroccan agri-food sector. For more than 50 years, data on the consumption of diesel fuel have been taken on a sample of 28 vehicles of different brands with a GVWR of 3, 5 tons up to 40 tons, the tracking operation by Global Positioning System (GPS), and Tachograph disk was essential in the speed and acceleration recording stage. For this, tracking two trailers of 19 tons and 40 tons is enough.

The purpose of this section is to assess the impact of a combination of factors on energy consumption with dynamic traffic conditions. On the basis of the results obtained, we can deduce the nature of the instantaneous emissions.

12.3   METHODOLOGY

12.3.1   Mesoscopic Modeling

In order to estimate emissions, three different approaches have been defined in recent years: macroscopic, mesoscopic, and microscopic.

The macroscopic view is an overall panoramic view of the entire logistics chain of the company, based on knowledge of the company's fleet vehicle, delivery quantities, subcontracting of means of transport, alliance strategy with other companies, and the use of global network parameters such as the values of the slope of the road, the nature of the journey, etc. [4–6].

The accuracy of this view is low, because no information is taken into account concerning the characteristics and the specific power of each vehicle, the speed, the loading rate, the acceleration time, the deceleration time, etc. For this reason, the minimization of energy consumption does not simply depend on the macroscopic approach; there are other factors related to vehicles, to driver behavior, and to the road and climate that are much more relevant to take into account.

The mesoscopic view is a reduced view compared to the macroscopic view, focused on a targeted process, builds synthetic training cycles, and is an interesting alternative to microscopic models if detailed data on speed and acceleration are not available [7].

The microscopic view can significantly improve the emission estimate, but it is generally applied to a subset of network links (100 km) because it requires a large amount of input data [8].

The linear relationship between two variables is usually explained by a linear regression model [9]. Linear regression was the first type of regression analysis to be rigorously studied and used extensively in many practical applications. So, at the mesoscopic level, we chose to evoke the model 1, which reflects the impact of the vehicle class on energy consumption, and model 2 which explains the impact of FP, age, GVWR, and EW.

Finally, in the microscopic view, we generated the model 3, which is interested in studying the impact of speed and acceleration on fuel consumption; these two parameters reflect the impact of driver behavior on consumption without forgetting obviously the social aspect in the control of the traffic standards and the management of the risks of the road.

12.3.1.1 Mesoscopic Factors Affecting Energy Consumption

The Pearson (ρ) factors of GVWR, FP, and EW successively presented in Table 12.1 are ($\rho_{GVWR} = 0.963$), ($\rho_{FP} = 0.954$), and ($\rho_{EW} = 0.961$), and they show the level of impact of each variable on consumption. The values of $\rho > 0.7$ are close to the correlation line, which indicates a strong linear relationship between the variables, whereas the Vehicle Age ($\rho_{Age} = 0.121$) has a low correlation coefficient, which us allows to neglect this variable in future considerations.

Bivariate correlation analysis and multiple regression analysis have been applied throughout this section; however, the bivariate correlation analysis reflects how the two variables are correlated, but the presence of a strong correlation between two variables does not assert a causal relation. To check if there is a cause-and-effect relationship between the variables, we must take into account the effects of the independent variables, and this is done by multiple regression analysis.

A multiple regression model is a linear model with multiple predictors or regressors [10]. The purpose of multiple regression is to learn more about the relationship between several independent variables and a dependent variable. In general, multiple regression analysis allows the researchers to ask the following question: What is the best predictor of…?

Also, the multiple regression analysis allows us to integrate the variation of several variables in the same analysis and to isolate the effects of single independent variables.

In this section, we will analyze the quality of the obtained models (1 and 2) through the study of the R or R-squared indicator and the F test, which helps us to compare the predicted values of the dependent variable with the real values.

The values of R and R-square are between 0 and 1, the value of R-square is important, and the model explains the phenomenon. In our case, the R-square of model 1 is 0.927 and of model 2 is 0.988, which means that the explanatory variables of models 1 and 2 contribute 92.7% and 98.8%, successively to the variable to explain, namely energy consumption. In general, if the R-square value is greater than 0.3, we can confirm the results.

TABLE 12.1
Correlation between Variables

		Ratio (L/100 km)	GVWR (T)	Age	FP	EW(T)
	Ratio (L/100 km)	1.000	0.963	0.121	0.954	0.961
	GVWR (T)	0.963	1.000	0.085	0.965	0.899
Pearson	Age	0.121	0.085	1.000	0.032	0.212
correlation (ρ)	FP	0.954	0.965	0.032	1.000	0.900
	EW (T)	0.961	0.899	0.212	0.900	1.000

TABLE 12.2
The Contribution of Different Predictors

			Standard	Edit Statistics			
Models	R	R-Squared	R-Squared Adjusted	Estimation Error	R-Squared Variation	F Variation	Sig of F Variation	Durbin–Watson
1	0.963[a]	0.927	0.924	2.41	0.927	340.519	0.000	
2	0.988[b]	0.976	0.972	1.46	0.049	16.288	0.000	2.022

[a] Predictors: (Constant), GVWR (T)
[b] Predictors: (Constant), GVWR (T), Age, **EW(T)**, FP

The R-squared values for both models show good explanatory and predictive capabilities of the models according to Table 12.2. Whether the most recent contribution shows a significant improvement in the prediction capacity of the regression equation, we must see the value of the variation of F and its significance value. In both the models, we notice that the variation of F is very significant, which allows us to say that the regression equation is significant and the explanatory variables contribute very significantly to the ratio variable scores (L/100 km) of energy consumption.

Before moving on to standardized regression coefficients, one has to analyze the model validity through the examination of residues, more particularly the Durbin–Watson test (DW), and the examination of graphs, for that the last column of Table 12.2 presents this test.

The test (DW) is used to evaluate the relationship between the residues and the errors. The test value varies between 0 and 4, and it will confirm or invalidate the hypothesis of independence between the residues to ensure that the residues are not correlated. It is necessary that the value of test of DW is close to 2, that is, to say in absolute value between 1.50 and 2.50. In our case, the DW test indicates a value of 2.022; this is a limit value in the safety interval that confirms that the residuals are not correlated and that the regression model is valid.

Following the mesoscopic analysis of the consumption of vehicles, models 1 and 2 help to predict the consumption envisaged, and at this level, the decision to purchase a new vehicle or subcontracting and route choices are essentially related to the technical characteristics of the vehicle, which can increase or decrease the consumption according to the strategic decision taken.

After the validation of the models, we will analyze the relationship between the explanatory variables and the variable to be explained through the standardized regression coefficient Beta, student test, and significance test. Table 12.3 contains the Beta regression coefficients, student test, and significance test. The standardized Beta coefficient is interpreted in the same way as the Pearson regression coefficient, so if Beta is less than the absolute value of 0.29, the effect is low; if Beta's absolute value is between 0.3 and 0.49, the effect is medium; and if Beta is greater than the absolute value of 0.5, the effect is strong. Student's T test is used to test the significance of a regression coefficient. In Table 12.3, the coefficients show that the vehicle

TABLE 12.3

The Functions of the Multiple Regression Models 1 and 2

	Models	Unstandardized Coefficients		Standardized Coefficients	t	Sig.
		B	Standard Error	Beta		
1	(Constant)	14.744	0.706		20.895	0.000
	GVWR (T)	0.550	0.030	0.963	18.453	0.000
2	(Constant)	8.260	1.531		5.394	0.000
	GVWR (T)	0.232	0.072	0.406	3.195	0.004
	Age	−0.032	0.052	−0.022	−0.625	0.538
	FP	0.119	0.134	0.118	0.891	0.382
	EW(T)	2.188	0.706	0.494	6.033	0.000

GVWR for model 1 has a large effect on consumption and for model 2 the GVWR and EW have a significant effect with a p-value <0.01; however the Age and the FP do not have a significant impact. In summary, the highest Beta coefficient has a big impact on the energy consumption.

After taking into account all of these aspects, the regression analysis was carried out to evolve models 1 and 2 with its four parameters, the estimated coefficients, and the associated statistics that are displayed in Table 12.3.

The prediction according to model 2 ($R^2 = 0.9758$) compared to model 1 ($R^2 = 0.927$) is closer to reality according to Figure 12.1, so, the consumption is not simply related to the vehicle weight, but there are other vehicle characteristics that influence the consumption on the road.

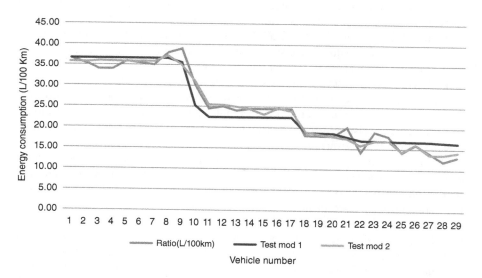

FIGURE 12.1 Model deviations from the actual model.

The nonstandardized coefficients allow us to reconstruct the equation of the regression line of models 1 and 2, so in this case, the following equations are construed:

Model 1: $Y_1 = 0.55 \times GVWR + W\ 14.744$

Model 2: $Y_2 = 0.232 \times GVWR + 0.119 \times FP + 2.188 \times EW - 0.032 \times Age + 8.260$

12.3.1.2 Microscopic Factors Affecting Energy Consumption

According to Wisetjindawat et al. [11], microscopic modeling aims to collect data parameters such as flow, density, speed, travel time, long queues, stops, pollution, fuel consumption, and shock waves. The characteristics of this modeling were based on the vehicle tracking models, the lane change models, and the causes of disruption of individual drivers [12, 13].

The database used is recovered from a Moroccan industrial company with a fleet of vehicles. These data allow the study of the impact of the vehicle class GVWR, EW, FP, and age with the models 1 and 2, as well as the speed and acceleration with model 3, according to Table 12.4.

Fuel consumption and emissions are strictly related to speed and acceleration profiles that often depend on two categories of parameters: traffic conditions and driving behavior.

The first category includes the maximum speed limit and the theoretical acceleration rate, which vary according to the characteristics of the infrastructure, the actual speed, the acceleration rate, and the number of vehicles that stop due to congestion and the flow of the road network. The second category considers the different driving behaviors of the users; from a physical point of view, driving behavior is represented by speed-time and acceleration-time charts.

Analyzing the entire fleet vehicle is not obvious because of time consumed and the variety of behaviors of drivers, which can generate more error in the development of model 3; for this reason, the registration of 118 catches of two categories of vehicles ($V_1 = 19$ tons and $V_2 = 40$ tons) is sufficient to provide a multivariable function (speed, acceleration) showing the level of impact of each factor on energy consumption and CO_2 emissions.

TABLE 12.4
Summary of Model 3

Model	R	R-Squared	R-Squared Adjusted	Standard Error of Estimate	R-Squared Variation	F Variation	Sig. of F Variation	Durbin–Watson
					Edit Statistics			
3	0.812[a]	0.659	0.650	1.74243%	0.659	73.343	0.000	0.950

[a] Predictors: (Constant), γ (m/s^{-2}), Vmax (km/h), GVWR (T).

TABLE 12.5
The Multivariable Function of Model 3

	Model	Unstandardized Coefficients		Standardized Coefficients		
		B	Standard Error	Beta	t	Sig.
3	(Constant)	30.540	1.055		28.938	0.000
	GVWR (T)	0.278	0.023	0.981	12.223	0.000
	Vmax (km/h)	−0.057	0.016	−0.276	−3.510	0.001
	γ (m²/s)	6.168	21.610	0.016	0.285	0.776

To achieve this plan, speed optimization has become a typical way to improve fuel efficiency, as it would reduce engine power or fuel consumption three times faster [14].

The linear relationship between a response variable and several predictors is explained by several linear regressions, However, in many practical applications, multiple predictors may be associated with a response variable [15].

Multiple regression analysis was considered as a way to describe the relationship between energy consumption and a plurality of predictors (GVWR, speed, and acceleration); this relationship can help predict the response variable (energy consumption) according to Table 12.5.

The general formula obtained in the microscopic level is:

$$Y_3 = 30,545 + 0.278 \times GVWR - 0.057 \times Vmax + 0.168 \times \gamma \qquad (12.1)$$

12.4   RESULTS AND DISCUSSION

Macroscopic modeling describes intersections at a low level of details [12], similar to the discussion in Demir [16] that speed has a significant effect on fuel consumption, and an optimal speed could lead to improved reduction of CO_2 emissions.

According to articles from authors [5, 17–20] the effect of driver behavior on diesel fuel consumption, engine types, speed, and acceleration were considered the main factors; thus, transport-related CO_2 emissions are affected by various vehicle type conditions (engine power, torque, fuel type, aerodynamic drag coefficient, etc.), the characteristics of the delivery operation (type of road, slope, vehicle speed, load, etc.) [21], psychological factors of the driver (personality traits) [22], attitudes and intentions [23], and risk taking [24] in studies dealing with fuel savings and emission reductions. In addition, other variables also affecting CO_2 emissions include traffic, driving style [25], and weather conditions [26].

Validation of models 1 and 2 were performed between the predicted regression equations for predicted consumption and measured consumption according to Figure 12.2 and Figure 12.3 (mod 1 test and mod 2 test). To test the regression

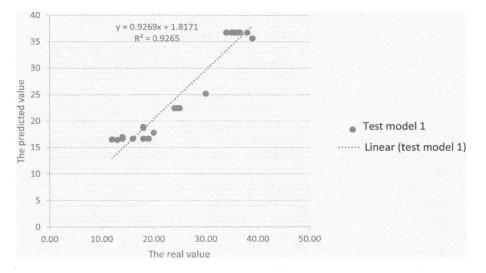

FIGURE 12.2 Predicted values compared with the real values according to model 1.

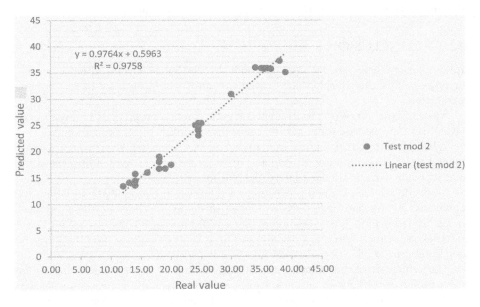

FIGURE 12.3 Predicted values versus real values by model 2.

equations, validation was performed by multiple correlation for 28 types of vehicles. From the result obtained, the regression equation predicted by model 1 gave a strong $R^2 = 0.9265$, so model 2 is getting the $R^2 = 0.9265$ to $R^2 = 0.9758$; this variation of 0.0493 appears significant.

The high correlation confirmed that the predicted fuel consumption was reliable and efficient, indicating that the expected consumption of the multiple linear regression was similar, accurate, and efficient, confirming that the fuel consumption predicted by the multiple linear regression was similar to the measured one.

Model 3 presents $R^2 = 0.659$ that is less than model 2 with $R^2 = 0.9758$, which shows that variables such as acceleration and speed generate noisy and unstable environmental conditions if taken into consideration.

When comparing the fuel consumption of a quiet motorist and an aggressive driver, who drives too fast, accelerates more than necessary, brakes suddenly, changes gears continuously, etc., we can obtain a difference up to 20% on the road and 40% in the city according to [27, 28].

Model 3 is related to the type of transmission, as it was mentioned the optimality can be achieved with an automatic transmission of speed not to leave room for unnecessary changes on the part of the driver.

This model is less controllable, that is to say the vehicle fleet manager can educate drivers by offering training, for example. However, he will never be able to fully control the driving behavior on the road.

The type of driver is unfortunately not considered in any of the existing calculation methods because of its difficulty to control a dynamic agent.

12.5   CONCLUSION

Regression analysis can be used for both forecasting and controlling a product or process characteristic that is essential to quality based on a set of key process parameters.

Although the use of regression analysis for prediction purposes is highly responsive, this is not the case for controlling process variables.

When planning a trip, it is essential to find the best route to take based on environmental conditions, condition of vehicles, driver, tonnage, destination infrastructure, and schedule, which influence safety and real-time travel.

Controlled vehicles already constitute a relatively large database in which the conditions of use and operation are known in detail. In addition, these vehicles, being "in circulation," are an excellent "sensor" for measuring traffic conditions.

Analysis of their speed profiles allowed to us to describe to some extent driving conditions and vehicle flow, considering the diversity of driver behavior.

The vehicle driver has a major role in minimizing the emissions recorded in the same period of traffic with the same category of vehicle. Making a sustainable optimization of road transport of goods is a combination of the strategic decision of transport manager and an operational decision carrier.

The strategic decision is ensured by the choice of the optimal route in terms of safety, speed, and cost. On the other hand, the operational decision is directly related to the carrier behavior related to its responsiveness, acceleration, deceleration, braking and concentration code compliance of the road, and the transmission of information to the actors of the chain when it is necessary.

REFERENCES

[1] A. Shukla and M. Alum, "Assessment of real world on-road vehicle emissions under dynamic urban traffic conditions in Delhi," *International Journal of Urban Sciences*, vol. 14, no. 2, pp. 207–220, 2010.

[2] S. Carrese, A. Gemma, and S. La Spada, "Impacts of driving behaviours, slope and vehicle load factor on bus fuel consumption and emissions: A real case study in the city of Rome," *Procedia—Social and Behavioral Sciences*, vol. 87, pp. 211–221, 2013.

[3] W. Ech-Chelfi and M. El Hammoumi, "Survey on the relation between road freight transport, SCM and sustainable development," *Yugoslav Journal of Operations Research*, vol. 29, no. 2, pp. 151–176, 2019.

[4] S. M. R. Dente and L. Tavasszy, "Policy oriented emission factors for road freight transport," *Transportation Research Part D: Transport and Environment*, 2017, vol. 61, pp. 33–41.

[5] N. H. Muslim, A. Keyvanfar, A. Shafaghat, M. M. Abdullahi, and M. Khorami, "Green driver: Travel behaviors revisited on fuel saving and less emission," *Sustainability*, vol. 10, no. 2, pp. 1–30, 2018.

[6] W. Ech-Chelfi and M. EL Hammoumi, "Development of the Java-based Dijkstra algorithm for optimal path detection," *Journal of Engineering and Applied Sciences*, vol. 14, no. 18, pp. 6620–6624, 2019.

[7] H. Yue, H. Rakha, "Validation of the VT-Meso vehicle fuel consumption and emission model," *Efficient Transportation and Pavement Systems: Characterization Mechanisms, Simulation, and Modeling*, p. 97, 2008.

[8] C. Samaras, D. Tsokolis, S. Toffolo, G. Magra, L. Ntziachristos, and Z. Samaras, "Improving fuel consumption and CO2 emissions calculations in urban areas by coupling a dynamic micro traffic model with an instantaneous emissions model," *Transportation Research Part D: Transport and Environment*, vol. 65, pp. 772–783, 2018.

[9] P. S. Mann, *Introductory statistics*, John Wiley & Sons, Hoboken, NJ, 2007.

[10] R. B. Darlington and A. F. Hayes, "Regression analysis and linear models: Concepts, application and implementation," 2016.

[11] W. Wisetjindawat, K. Yamamoto, and F. Marchal, "A commodity distribution model for a multi-agent freight system," *Procedia—Social and Behavioral Sciences*, vol. 39, pp. 534–542, 2012.

[12] N. N. Nor Azlan and M. Md Rohani, "Overview of application of traffic simulation model," *MATEC Web of Conferences*, vol. 150, p. 03006, 2018.

[13] M. Barth, T. Youngslove, and G. Scora, "Development of a heavy-duty diesel modal emissions and fuel consumption model," *PATH Research Report*, no. January, p. 113, 2005.

[14] S. Wang, B. Ji, J. Zhao, W. Liu, and T. Xu, "Predicting ship fuel consumption based on LASSO regression," *Transportation Research Part D: Transport and Environment*, vol. 65, pp. 817–824, 2018.

[15] E. Demir, T. Bektaş, and G. Laporte, "A comparative analysis of several vehicle emission models for road freight transportation," *Transportation Research Part D: Transport and Environment*, vol. 16, no. 5, pp. 347–357, 2011.

[16] E. Demir, T. Bektaş, and G. Laporte, "An adaptive large neighborhood search heuristic for the pollution-routing problem," *European Journal of Operational Research*, vol. 223, no. 2, pp. 346–359, 2012.

[17] J. Chung, Y. Kyung, and J. Kim, "Optimal sustainable road plans using multi-objective optimization approach," *Transport Policy*, vol. 49, pp. 105–113, 2016.

[18] E. Demir, T. Bektas, and G. Laporte, "A review of recent research on green road freight transportation," *European Journal of Operational Research*, vol. 237, no. 3, pp. 775–793, 2014.

[19] M. Baumgartner, J. Léonardi, and O. Krusch, "Improving computerized routing and scheduling and vehicle telematics: A qualitative survey," *Transportation Research Part D: Transport and Environment*, vol. 13, no. 6, pp. 377–382, 2008.

[20] W. Ech-Chelfi and M. El Hammoumi, "The impact level of the environmental approach on Moroccan industries: Case study," *International Journal of Engineering Research and Technology*, vol. 12, no. 2, pp. 172–179, 2019.

[21] R. Akçelik and M. Besley, "Operating cost, fuel consumption, and emission models in aaSIDRA and aaMOTION," *ResearchGate*, no. March 2014, 2003.

[22] D. Jovanović, K. Lipovac, P. Stanojević, and D. Stanojević, "The effects of personality traits on driving-related anger and aggressive behaviour in traffic among Serbian drivers," *Transportation Research Part F: Traffic Psychology and Behaviour*, vol. 14, no. 1, pp. 43–53, 2011.

[23] F. Lucidi, L. Mallia, L. Lazuras, and C. Violani, "Personality and attitudes as predictors of risky driving among older drivers," *Accident Analysis and Prevention*, vol. 72, pp. 318–324, 2014.

[24] X. Cai, J. J. Lu, Y. Xing, C. Jiang, and W. Lu, "Analyzing driving risks of roadway traffic under adverse weather conditions: In case of rain day," *Procedia—Social and Behavioral Sciences*, vol. 96, pp. 2563–2571, 2013.

[25] Alan McKinnon, Sharon Cullinane, M. Browne, and A. Whiteing, "Green logistics: Improving the environmental sustainability of logistics, 2010.

[26] C. Kohn, "Centralisation of distribution systems and its environmental effects," no. 91, 2005.

[27] Agence de l'environnement et de la maîtrise de l'énergie, "Consommations conventionnelles de carburant et émissions de CO2," Guide édité en application du décret no 2002-1508 du 23 décembre 2002, relatif à l'information sur la consommation de carburant et les émissions de dioxyde de carbone des voitures particulières neuves., p. 353, 2018.

[28] M. P. Trépanier and L. C. Coelho, "Facteurs et méthodes de calcul d'émissions de gaz à effet de serre," *Centre interuniversitaire de recherche sur les réseaux d'entreprise, la logistique et le transport (CIRRELT)*, 2017.

13 Impact of Limescale on Home Appliances in a Building

Hajji Abdelghani, Ahmed Abbou, and El Boukili Abdellah
Mohamed V University, Rabat, Morocco

CONTENTS

13.1 INTRODUCTION

Energy efficiency of buildings is a hot topic. In Morocco, a lot of researchers are interested in this topic because buildings are the biggest energy consumer before transportation and industry. It also represents 25% of national carbon dioxide emissions. [Abarkan, 2014]

Energy efficiency is considered today the fourth-largest energy source after fossil fuels, renewable energies, and nuclear energy. The ambition of the Kingdom of Morocco is to ensure a better use of energy in all areas of economic and social activity, considering the need to rationalize and decrease the consumption of energy to meet the growing energy needs of our country. [Law 47-09 on Energy efficiency, 2015]

Buying economical household appliances is not sufficient, since much of the electrical consumption of a piece of equipment depends on how it is used and maintained throughout its life. [ADEREE, (n.d.)]

The phenomenon of limescale formation occurs in cold water urban distribution systems and more intensively in the heat transport circuits of industrial plants and in hydraulic devices that produce or use hot water.

The technological and economic consequences of scaling are varied:

- Loss of efficiency due to the insulating power of limescale, which increases the energy consumption (10 mm of limestone on the electrical resistance can increase losses up to 50%). [ASPEC SERVIGAZ, (n.d.)]
- Shortening of the life of the already expensive equipment.
- Rise in the temperature of the appliances with the risk of destruction by overheating.
- The malfunction of the hydraulic devices.
- A progressive reduction of the pipe sections with an increase of pressure losses or even their obstruction.
- In addition, tartar in large quantities is an agent promoting the development of certain bacteria such as *Legionella*. [Hadfi, 2012]

Our research work, conducted by the Mohammadia School of Engineering (Mohamed V University of Rabat), begins with the measurement of the hardness of drinking water in four regions in Morocco. Then, we try to find, theoretically, the conditions that minimize the quantity of limescale in hot water considering the comfort and health of the occupants of the building.

Subsequently, we will show experimentally that drinking water which contains the higher quantity of limescale (higher TH) will require more energy to heat.

Finally, we will lead a comparative study about the energy consumption of the various hydraulic devices of a building using different waters.

13.2 RELATED WORK

There are very few published research reports on the energy impact of limestone on home appliances.

Lerato Lethea (2017) has studied the impact of water hardness on the energy consumption of geyser heating elements. That study proved that the scale formation of 1.5 kW and 3 kW geyser heating elements because of high total water hardness that raised the energy consumption by about 4% to 12%. It proposed an energy-efficient electronic descaling technology. In my opinion, it is a good thing, but it is necessary to act before the scale is left in large quantities. We suggest, therefore, a softener which slows down scaling.

On the other hand, Konstadinos Abeliotis (2015) studied the impact of water hardness on consumers' perception of laundry in five European countries. He showed that the hardness of water is a key factor in the success of the washing process. For the first time, a research study was conducted in five European countries that aimed at identifying consumers' perceptions about the effect of water hardness in washing performances. The results indicate that satisfaction with the washing result depends on the hardness of water.

In the same study, we observe that the use of softened drinking water in households has several positive effects, such as the reduction in energy consumption.

In the same context, Bruce A. Cameron (2011) worked on consumers' detergent considerations: hard water laundering—How much additional detergent is needed?

He showed that liquid detergents wash in both fresh and hard water. Powdered detergents were more efficient than liquids in fresh water. The hardness of water affected powdered detergents and, depending on the type of detergent, 10% to 15% to over 30% additional detergent was needed to achieve a similar result to that of fresh water.

Additionally, researchers studied the effect of all appliances that use hot water.

13.3   WATER HARDNESS MEASUREMENT

We will begin this work by measuring experimentally the hardness of drinking water in four regions of Morocco. The hardness, called the hydrotimetric title (TH), corresponds to the totality of the calcium and magnesium salts:

$$TH = \left[Ca^{2+} \right] + \left[Mg^{2+} \right] \tag{13.1}$$

13.3.1   EQUIPMENT

The equipment that has been used in this study is the material that allows the experimental determination of the TH hardness of water:

drop sensor—LabQuest interface—Eriochrome black T (NET) —
tetra-acetic ethylene diamine (EDTA) —buffer solution 5 mL —
Erlenmeyer 250 mL—magnetic stirrer and stir bar.

13.3.2 METHOD

The method to determine the total hardness of water is based on complexation assays to form very stable complexes between a central ion (calcium, magnesium) and an EDTA ligand.

In a 250-mL Erlenmeyer flask, $V_{water} = 50$ mL of drinking water to be analyzed is added, 5 mL of the buffer solution and one drop of NET indicator are added, and then, the mixture is titrated with EDTA solution. The shift is reached when we see the royal blue color.

The equivalence relation is written as:

$$[EDTA].V_{eq} = \left(\left[Ca^{2+}\right] + \left[Mg^{2+}\right]\right).V_{water} \qquad (13.2)$$

V_{eq} is volume of equivalence.

It is shown that the TH in French degree unit, noted °F, is written as:

$$TH = 5.08.V_{eq}\,(mL) \qquad (13.3)$$

13.3.3 RESULTS

The results obtained for the samples from four regions in Morocco are presented in Table 13.1.

13.3.4 DISCUSSION

Water hardness depends on where you live and on the soil geology of your area. This is why it is important to be well informed on this subject; otherwise, you will deal with a lot of inconveniences caused by limescale. [Union française des profession-nels du traitement de l'eau, (n.d.)]

Limescale is naturally present in water. Its presence in small or large quantities depends on the nature of the terrain crossed. In Table 13.1, it can be seen that water E1 is hardest. It contains the higher quantity of limescale compared to the waters of the other regions. Water E4 is the softest.

Hard water causes scaling of distribution networks and excessive consumption of detergent; fresh water can cause the pipes to corrode. So, water hardness should be moderated to ensure an acceptable balance between corrosion and scaling. [Sante Canada, 1979]

TABLE 13.1
TH Values of Four Regions in Morocco

Water Sample	E1	E2	E3	E4
TH in °F	41.60	28.48	28.00	10.24
Nature of water	Very hard	Hard	Hard	Soft

13.4   STUDY OF THE EFFECT OF TEMPERATURE AND PH ON LIMESCALE FORMATION

We will study theoretically limescale dissolution according to temperature T and pH.

13.4.1   MATERIAL

In this study we will use MATLAB® software.

13.4.2   METHOD

To study limescale dissolution at temperature T and pressure p, it is assumed that:

- Limescale is assimilated to calcium carbonate $CaCO_3(s)$.
- The liquid phase is in equilibrium with the gas phase with respect to carbon dioxide exchanges.
- The ions' activities are almost equal to the ions' molar concentrations. [Cortial, (n.d.)]

The following reactions come into play:

$$CaCO_3\,(s) = Ca^{2+} + CO_3^{2-}\,\left(K_S:\text{ solubility product}\right)$$

$$CO_2 + 2H_2O = HCO^- + H_3O^+\,\left(K_{a1}:\text{ acidity constant 1}\right)$$

$$HCO^- + H_2O = CO_3^{2-} + H_3O^+\,\left(K_{a2}:\text{ acidity constant 2}\right)$$

The solubility S of calcium carbonate is defined by [Cortial, (n.d.)]:

$$S = \left[CO_2\right] + \left[HCO^-\right] + \left[CO_3^{2-}\right] \tag{13.4}$$

We can show that:

$$S = \left(10^{X-2.pH} + 10^{Y-pH} + 10^{-Z}\right)^{0.5} \tag{13.5}$$

Where, $X = pK_{a1} + pK_{a2} - pK_S$
$Y = pK_{a2} - pK_S$
$Z = pK_S$

13.4.3   RESULTS

The numerical values of the parameters for different temperatures are presented in Table 13.2. [Cortial, (n.d.)]

TABLE 13.2
Values of Parameters

T(°C)	pK$_{a1}$	pK$_{a2}$	pK$_S$	X	Y	Z
0	6.83	10.63	8.022	9.191	2.608	8.022
25	6.368	10.33	8.341	8.357	1.989	8.341
50	6.296	10.17	8.625	7.841	1.545	8.625
75	6.186	9.99	8.862	7.314	1.128	8.862

Figure 13.1 shows the representation of the solubility as a function of pH for different temperatures in the MATLAB environment.

13.4.4 DISCUSSION

Temperature has a significant influence on the solubility of calcium carbonate. The latter increases the presence of carbon dioxide. Indeed, the increase in temperature decreases the amount of dissolved carbon dioxide and causes the precipitation of calcium carbonate. [Hadfi, 2012]

From Figure 13.1 we notice that pH rise favors the formation of limescale, and the increase in temperature favors the precipitation of calcium carbonate. To minimize the quantity of the formed limescale and ensure comfort to the occupants, you should thus adjust your appliances to moderated temperatures between 55°C and 60°C, and the water pH should be between 6.5 and 7. [Health Ministry, 2006]

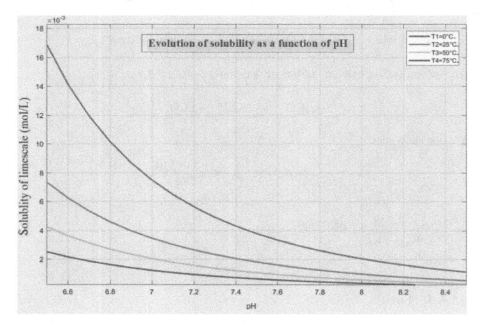

FIGURE 13.1   Solubility of limescale as a function of pH for different temperatures.

13.5 EVOLUTION OF THE ENERGY SUPPLIED TO WATER ACCORDING TO TEMPERATURE

We will study the evolution of the energy supplied to water as a function of temperature for different TH values.

13.5.1 EQUIPMENT

Here is the material that makes this study possible:

calorimeter—temperature sensor—LabQuest chain acquisition—computer—resistor 3Ω—four drinking water samples—graduated cylinder—6-V voltage generator—multimeter—magnetic stirrer and stir bar—connection wires.

13.5.2 METHOD

Figure 13.2 shows the experimental setup.
The energy supplied to the water is calculated using the following relation:

$$E = R.I^2.\Delta t \tag{13.6}$$

Where, R is electrical resistance.

I is current intensity (A).
Δt is required duration.

We repeated the experiment for the other samples.

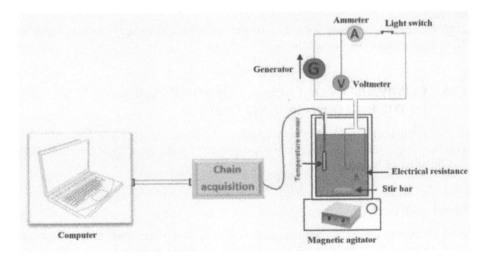

FIGURE 13.2 Experimental device.

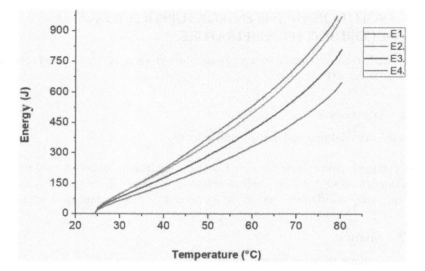

FIGURE 13.3   Evolution of energy supplied to water as a function of temperature T.

13.5.3   RESULTS

Figure 13.3 shows the obtained experimental results.

13.5.4   DISCUSSION

In Figure 13.3, the curves do not evolve in the same way because of the water hardness. Indeed, the harder the water, the more energy is required to get to the apparatus' temperature of use.

Consequently, drinking water E4 (harder) requires more energy to heat water at the temperature of use of the device.

13.6   COMPARISON OF ENERGY CONSUMPTION IN THE BUILDING IN TWO CASES

In this comparative study, we will estimate the annual energy consumed by the hydraulic apparatus of our building in two extreme cases: water E4 of hardness TH4 and water E1 of hardness TH1.

13.6.1   DEVICES

We looked at the domestic appliances of a four-person house: dishwasher, washing machine, electric kettle, electric water heater, and coffee maker.

13.6.2 Method

The energy required to heat a volume V of water from temperature T_1 to temperature T_2 per cycle of each apparatus is calculated using the following relation:

$$E_{cycle} = R.I^2.\Delta t.V/V_0 \qquad (13.7)$$

Where, V is volume of water used by the device during a cycle.
V_0 is volume of water used during the experiment.

Annual energy is deducted for each device by inducing the frequency of use:

$$E_{annual} = 365.f.R.I^2.\Delta t.V/V_0 \qquad (13.8)$$

Where, f is frequency of use of the device per day.

13.6.3 Results

In Table 13.3, we can read the appliances of a four-person house.

13.6.4 Discussion

It is confirmed that the annual consumption for hard water is higher. The relative difference between the two previous energies is written as $\Delta E/E = 38.85\%$. More than 38% of the energy consumption of a building's hydraulic equipment can be reduced if E4 water is used instead of E1 water. We note that with fresh water we consume

---

TABLE 13.3
Appliances' Annual Consumption

Character Appliances	Volume of Water/Cycle	Operating T (°C)	Frequency of Use(D⁻¹)[a]	Consumed Annual Energy in MJ	
				Water E4	Water E1
Dishwasher	20 L	50	1	11.33	19.33
Washing machine	50 L	40	0.5	9.16	14.16
Electric kettle	1 L	100	4	12	18.93
Coffee maker	0.5 L	100	1	1.50	2.36
Electric water heater	80 L	60	2	133.33	218.66

Note: Total annual energy for E4 is 46.38 kWh. Total annual energy for E1 is 75.85 kWh
[a] Average values were derived from the devices' catalogs.

less energy, thus it reduces the electricity bill of our building. Further, the reduction of limescale in water also extends the life of our devices and reduces the frequency of maintenance of these devices.

13.7 CONCLUSION

The results show that it is preferable to introduce a water filtering system (softener), especially in areas where water is hard or very hard. This will be applied to the building's water supply to reduce the energy bill, extend the life of hydraulic installations, reduce the frequency of maintenance, make soap and detergents more efficient, and improve the quality of drinking water.

To ensure the energy efficiency of buildings, it is necessary to do the following:

• Know the TH of drinking water used in the building.
• Know the effects of parameters that favor the formation of limescale.
• Choose the class of devices used in the buildings.
• Properly use and adjust devices.
• Install a softener, etc.

13.8 PERSPECTIVES

• Studying the profitability of a softener in the same building.
• Analyzing the consequences of the replacement of an electric water heater by a solar one.

REFERENCES

Abarkan, M., 2014, *"Modélisation et Analyse du comportement d'un Bâtiment équipé d'un Système Multi Sources d''énergie"*, PhD Thesis, Aix University, Marseille and Sidi Mohamed Ben Abdellah University, Fes, Morocco.

Abeliotis, K., 2015, "Impact of water hardness on consumers' perception of laundry washing result in five European countries", International Journal of Consumer Studies, vol. 39, Harokopio University, Athens, Greece. Available at: https://onlinelibrary.wiley.com/doi/full/10.1111/ijcs.12149. Accessed: Oct 2018.

ADEREE, (n.d.) *"Les bonnes pratiques de l'efficacité énergétique des bâtiments"*. Available at: http://docplayer.fr/14141959-Les-bonnes-pratiques-de-l-efficacite-energetique-dans-le-batiment.html. Accessed: April 2018.

ASPEC SERVIGAZ, (n.d.), *"EMBOUAGE: Causes, Effets, et Résolutions de Problèmes"*. Available at: https://www.aspec-servigaz.fr/index.php/desembouage/causes-effets-et-resolution-de-lembouage. Accessed: April 2018.

Cameron, B. A., 2011, "Detergent considerations for consumers: Laundering in hard water—how much extra detergent is required?", Journal of Extension, vol. 49, no. 4, University of Wyoming Laramie, Wyoming. Available at: https://www.joe.org/joe/2011august/rb6.php. Accessed: Oct 2018.

Cortial, N. (n.d.), *"Précipitation—Produit de solubilité"*. Available at: http://nicole.cortial.net/complements/chimie/web-cours-pr%E9cipitation.pdf. Accessed: May 2018.

Hadfi, A., 2012, *"Evaluation du pouvoir entartrant des eauxdu secteur agricole du grand Agadir"*, PhD Thesis, Ibn Zohr University, Agadir, Morocco.

Health Ministry, 2006, *"Qualité des eaux d'alimentation humaine, Norme Marocaine homologuée"*, Morocco.

Law 47-09 on Energy efficiency, 2015. Available at: http://www.aust.ma/images/aust/reglementation/Dahirs/Dahir%201-11-161.pdf. Accessed: March 2018.

Lethea, L., 2017, "Impact of water hardness on energy consumption of geyser heating elements", Water, vol. 43, no. 4, Pretoria, Oct. 2017, South Africa. Available at: http://www.scielo.org.za/scielo.php?script=sci_arttext&pid=S1816-79502017000400009. Accessed: Oct 2018.

Sante Canada, 1979, *"Recommandations pour la qualité de l'eau potable au Canada: documenttechnique – la dureté"*. Available at: https://www.canada.ca/fr/sante-canada/services/publications/vie-saine/recommandations-pour-qualite-eau-potable-canada-document-technique-durete.html. Accessed: August 2018.

Union française des professionnels du traitement de l'eau, (n.d.), *"Tout sur le calcaire"*. Available at: http:www.uae.fr. Accessed: August 2018.

Index

Page numbers in *italics* refer to figures and those in **bold** refer to tables.